LIVING IN PROVENCE

Photos and texts by BARBARA and RENÉ STOELTIE et al.
Edited by ANGELIKA TASCHEN

TASCHEN

Bibliotheca Universalis

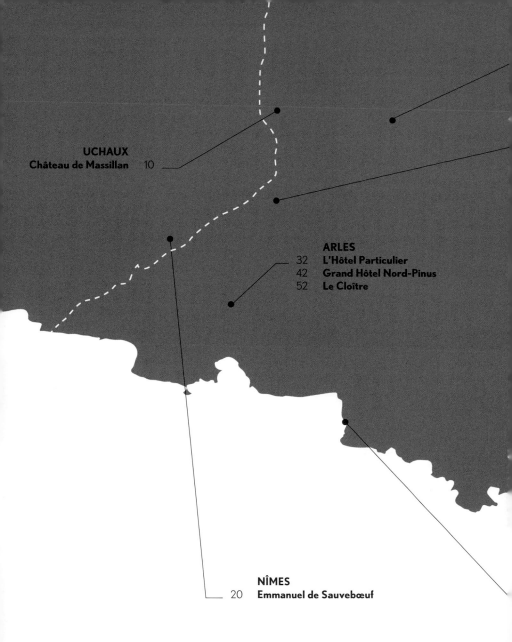

CONTENTS

CHÂTEAU DE MASSILLAN

CHÂTEAU DE MASSILLAN
DIDIER PERRÉOL
UCHAUX

Situated in the heart of the Rhône vineyards and at a convenient distance from the ancient city of Orange, the sturdy crenellated towers of Château de Massillan – which once belonged to Diane de Poitiers, mistress of King Henry II – loom before the enchanted visitor. Transformed into a luxury hotel about 20 years ago, redeemed and redecorated by Didier Perréol, founder and president of Ekibio (a leading organic producer), the hotel's ethos is based on feng shui and the organic lifestyle. With its 24 rooms and its geobiological restaurant, the château attracts visitors from all over the world to a simple yet elegant setting that is full of charm. "Luxury and respect for nature can speak the same language," says Perréol, and the Château de Massillan is a proof of this.

Im Herzen der Rhône-Weinberge, nahe der antiken Stadt Orange, erhebt sich das Château de Massillan. Es beeindruckt den Besucher mit wehrhaften Rundtürmen, von Zinnen bekrönt. Das Schloss gehörte einst Diane de Poitiers, einer Mätresse König Heinrichs II. Vor etwa 20 Jahren zu einem Luxushotel umgebaut, wurde es zwischenzeitlich von Didier Perréol erworben und neu eingerichtet. Der Gründer und Direktor der Firma Ekibio, einem führenden Hersteller von Bio-Produkten, hat das Hotel nach den Prinzipien des Feng-Shui und mit natürlichen Materialien ausgestattet. Gäste aus aller Welt schätzen das Haus mit seinen 24 Zimmern, den eleganten und charmanten Rahmen und nicht zuletzt das Restaurant mit regionaler biologischer Küche und eigenem Gemüsegarten. "Luxus und Respekt vor der Natur können eindeutig die gleiche Sprache sprechen", erklärt Perréol, und das Schloss ist der Beweis dafür.

Situé au cœur des vignobles du Rhône et à une distance agréable de l'antique cité d'Orange, le Château de Massillan avec ses robustes tours à créneaux qui appartenait jadis à Diane de Poitiers, maîtresse royale d'Henri II, surgit devant l'œil enchanté du visiteur. Transformé en hôtel de luxe il y a une vingtaine d'années, et racheté et redécoré par Didier Perréol, président fondateur d'Ekibio, société leader de produits biologiques, le principe de l'hôtel se base sur le feng shui et la Bio. Avec ses 24 chambres, son restaurant géo biologique et son potager bio, le château attire des visiteurs du monde entier dans un cadre simple et raffiné, plein de charme. « Le luxe et le respect de la nature peuvent parler la même langue » dit Perréol et le Château de Massillan en est la preuve.

PP. 10–11 Off-white walls and pale stone set off period furniture and modern sofas upholstered in simple shades. The owner has adopted an elegantly restrained colour scheme. • Gebrochen weiße Wände, heller Naturstein und gedämpfte Dekostoffe für die Bezüge von Stilmöbeln und modernen Sofas: Die gewählte Farbpalette ist von einzigartiger Schlichtheit. • Murs blanc cassé, pierres blondes et nuances discrètes des tissus qui recouvrent le mobilier de style et les canapés contemporains. La palette choisie est d'une sobriété exemplaire.

P. 13 In the stairwell, the wrought-iron wall sconces echo the design of the banister whose elegant filigree work curves gracefully up the stairs. • Die schmiedeeiserne Wandleuchte im Treppenhaus harmoniert mit dem filigranen Geländer an der Treppe zum ersten Stock. • Dans la cage d'escalier, l'applique en fer forgé fait écho à la superbe rampe qui orne l'escalier en pierre menant à l'étage.

← This spacious gallery, leading off the courtyard, is filled with rattan armchairs and miniature lemon trees, tastefully juxtaposed with a more classic style of antique furniture. • Auf der großen Veranda am Ende des Hofs wechseln sich Rattansessel und Zitronenbäumchen mit klassisch geschwungenen Sitzgruppen ab. • Dans la grande galerie située au fond de la cour, des fauteuils en rotin et des citronniers en pot alternent avec des fauteuils et des canapés aux formes classiques.

↑ This imposing castle, guarded by fortress-style walls and resonant with the spirit of Diane de Poitiers, will appeal to those of a romantic bent. • Schloss oder Festung? Der einstige Wohnsitz von Diane de Poitiers ist ein Traum für die Romantiker unter uns. • Ce château aux allures de forteresse, qui abrite le souvenir de Diane de Poitiers ne peut que plaire aux esprits romantiques.

↑ A sober black and white atmosphere for the dining room. The earlier decor by Peter Wylly and Birgit Israël had been designed not to distract the diners' attention from the haute cuisine. • Der Speiseraum in strengem Schwarz-Weiß. Diese frühe Deko-Idee stammt von Peter Wylly und Birgit Israël und ist darauf ausgelegt, nicht von der raffinierten Küche abzulenken. • Ambiance blanc et noir stricte pour la salle à manger. L'ancienne décoration réalisée par Peter Wylly et Birgit Israël avait été conçue pour ne pas distraire l'attention de la cuisine raffinée.

→ Bathed in natural light from the dining-room window, the dark curtains frame an elegant still life of earthenware soup tureens posed on a white linen tablecloth. • Am Fenster des Speisesaals umrahmen dunkle Vorhänge ein Stillleben aus Fayence-Suppenterrinen auf schneeweißem Leinentischtuch. • Près de la fenêtre de la salle à manger, les rideaux sombres se lèvent sur une nature morte composée d'une table drapée de lin blanc et de quelques soupières en faïence.

← The bedrooms, furnished with impeccable taste, exude the same understated luxury as 'hôtels particuliers' of the 1930s and 40s. But every effort has been made to assure 21st-century comfort. • Die liebevoll möblierten Zimmer verströmen eine Aura von Luxus und Diskretion, wie sie die großen privaten Palais der 1930er- und 40er-Jahre besaßen. Dabei wird natürlich jeglichem modernen Komfort Rechnung getragen. • Les chambres

meublées avec le plus grand soin possèdent l'ambiance luxueuse et discrète des grands hôtels particuliers des années 1930 et 40. Et le confort si cher aux hommes du 21e siècle.

↓ The simple, sober style of the furniture accentuates the architectural austerity and minimalist inspiration that is also in evidence in the bathrooms. Here, the ochre charms of Provence are kept to the exterior. • Die Schlichtheit des

Mobiliars unterstreicht die strenge Architektur. Der gleiche minimalistische Geschmack findet sich in den Bädern. Hier muss der ockergelbe Charme der Provence draußen vor der Tür warten. • Le dépouillement du mobilier accentue l'austérité de l'architecture. On retrouve la même inspiration minimaliste dans les salles de bains. Ici la Provence ocrée ne « chante » qu'au-delà de la fenêtre.

EMMANUEL DE SAUVEBŒUF

EMMANUEL DE SAUVEBŒUF
NÎMES

Many are those, over the centuries, who have succumbed to the timeless charm of Nîmes. It is not difficult to understand why Thomas Jefferson spent an entire day admiring the imposing architecture of the Maison Carrée. Nor why others, before and after the great statesman, have been seduced by the powerful combination of the southern French sun and the classic beauty of the town's ancient Roman relics. Antique dealer Emmanuel de Sauvebœuf is a man for whom beauty is a primordial consideration in life. So it was only natural he should build a house that makes the perfect backdrop for his superb collection of period furniture, paintings and objets d'art. De Sauvebœuf found his ideal setting in a quiet village just outside town. Visitors will be impressed by the house's austere façade and the absence of any superfluous ornamentation, and charmed by the typical Provençal garden. The antique dealer appears to have an innate talent for interior decor. He has created a skilful and harmonious mix of classical sculpture and antique furniture which stands as a tribute to French cabinet making. The ensemble is set off by a palette of agreeably subtle colours.

Seit jeher lassen sich immer wieder Menschen vom Charme der Stadt Nîmes betören. Auch ohne allzu viel Fantasie versteht man, warum Thomas Jefferson sich einen ganzen Tag Zeit für die imposante Maison Carrée nahm oder warum andere vor und nach ihm dem perfekten Zusammenspiel von provenzalischem Sonnenlicht und den Zeugen der römischen Antike verfallen sind. Für Menschen wie den Antiquitätenhändler Emmanuel de Sauvebœuf ist Schönheit oberstes Gebot. Da er alte Möbel, Gemälde und kostbare Dinge liebt und verkauft, ließ er sich ein Haus bauen, das für seine Schätze einen würdigen Rahmen bildet. Dieses entstand in einem ruhigen Dorf in der Nähe der Stadt. Die Besucher beeindruckt nicht nur der wunderschöne, typisch provenzalische Garten, sondern auch das streng wirkende Haus, welches vollkommen frei von überflüssigem Zierrat ist. De Sauvebœuf besitzt ein angeborenes Talent für Innenarchitektur: Ihm gelingt einfach alles. Mit leichter Hand vereint er antike Statuen und erlesene Stilmöbel, die den französischen Kunstschreinern zur Ehre gereichen, mit Porzellanfiguren und kostbarem Nippes. Das Ergebnis ist ein harmonisches, durch subtile Farben getragenes Ambiente.

Ils ont été nombreux au cours du temps à tomber sous le charme de Nîmes. Faut-il vraiment beaucoup d'imagination pour comprendre pourquoi Thomas Jefferson a passé toute une journée à contempler la silhouette imposante de la Maison Carrée ? Et pourquoi d'autres avant et après lui ont été séduits par la combinaison idéale du soleil de Provence et de la beauté classique des vestiges de l'Antiquité romaine ? L'antiquaire Emmanuel de Sauvebœuf est de ces hommes pour qui la beauté est une condition primaire. Il va de soi que cet amateur et marchand de meubles, de tableaux et d'objets de qualité a choisi de construire une maison digne de ses acquisitions. Il a créé la demeure qui lui convient dans un village calme, situé près de la ville. La maison fascine les visiteurs par son aspect sévère et dépouillé de tout ornement superflu ainsi que par son splendide jardin typiquement provençal. De Sauvebœuf peut se vanter également d'avoir un talent inné pour la décoration intérieure. Tout semble lui réussir. Avec une belle aisance, il a su marier harmonieusement une statuaire classique, de beaux meubles d'époque, qui font la gloire de l'ébénisterie française, et une palette de couleurs d'une subtilité remarquable.

PP. 20–21 Could you ever have guessed that this magnificent Provençal house and garden were built only in the 21st century? A miracle, indeed! · Kaum zu glauben, dass dieses typisch provenzalische Haus mit seinem Garten erst im 21. Jahrhundert entstanden ist. · Peut-on imaginer que cette belle maison provençale et son jardin ont vu le jour au 21ᵉ siècle ? Cela tient du miracle.

P. 23 Emmanuel de Sauvebœuf has created a romantic garden filled with olive trees, drystone walls and a profusion of greenery and potted plants. · Olivenbäume, Trockenmauern und eine Fülle von Beet- und Kübelpflanzen machen den Garten von Emmanuel de

Sauvebœuf so herrlich romantisch. · Des oliviers, des murs en pierre sèche et une profusion de plantes et de plantes en pot composent le jardin romantique d'Emmanuel de Sauvebœuf.

↑ In the entrance hall, Emmanuel has found the perfect spot to show off his treasures. These include a Louis XV chair and a collection of 17th-century paintings. · Im Entrée hat Emmanuel Platz für seine liebsten Schätze gefunden: einen Louis-XV-Sessel und Bilder aus dem 17. Jahrhundert. · Dans l'entrée, Emmanuel a trouvé une place de choix pour ses trésors : un siège Louis XV et des tableaux 17ᵉ.

→ The pale stone staircase is hung with engravings of Roman emperors and ecclesiastical figures. · Die Wände an der hellen Steintreppe sind mit zahlreichen Stichen von römischen Kaisern und Geistlichen bestückt. · La cage d'escalier en pierre blonde est tapissée de gravures représentant des empereurs romains et des ecclésiastiques.

↑ → and PP. 28–29 Emmanuel is an inveterate collector whose eclectic tastes range from neo-classical plaster statuettes and seashells to antique patchwork, religious icons and oil portraits. • Emmanuel ist Sammler aus Passion. Ob klassizistische Gipsbüsten, Muscheln, alte Patchworkdecken, Heiligenstatuen oder Porträts – ihn fasziniert alles. • Emmanuel est un collectionneur invétéré. Qu'il s'agisse de plâtres d'académie néo-classiques, de coquillages, d'anciens patchworks, de statues religieuses ou de portraits, tout l'enchante.

↑ The Louis XVI-kitchen is packed with jams and preserves. Traditional Provençal pottery adds a colourful, regional touch to the room. • In dem Louis-XVI-Wandschrank in der Küche verbergen sich unzählige Marmeladengläser. Provenzalische Fayencen geben dem Raum eine bodenständige Note. • Dans les placards de style Louis XVI de la cuisine s'entassent d'innombrables pots de confiture. Les faïences provençales ajoutent une note de couleur et de terroir.

→ The kitchen cupboards are a veritable treasure trove of homemade jams and preserves. • In den Küchenschränken reihen sich Gläser mit Eingemachtem und hausgemachter Konfitüre. • Les placards de la cuisine abritent des conserves et des confitures maison.

L'HÔTEL PARTICULIER

Poem of colors

The most remarkable abodes from Costa Careyes to the Yucatán Peninsula

Rustic wood, wrought iron, vibrant color, and tantalizing patterns: the homes of Mexico blend native tribal styles and Spanish architecture with warm, textured simplicity. Dive into inspiring and remarkable abodes in this updated, compact portfolio of villas, casitas, haciendas, cabanas, and palapas, featuring many unpublished images that paint a lively and colorful picture of Mexican style.

"...luscious pictures that burst with beautiful colours and exotic features."
—*Aspire Magazine*, London

LIVING IN MEXICO

Photos and texts by BARBARA & RENÉ STOELTIE
Edited by ANGELIKA TASCHEN

TASCHEN
Bibliotheca Universalis

Living in Mexico
Barbara & René Stoeltie, Angelika Taschen
432 pages
TRILINGUAL EDITIONS IN:
ENGLISH / DEUTSCH / FRANÇAIS &
ESPAÑOL / ITALIANO / PORTUGUÊS

Nippon nests

Today's most exceptional Japanese homes

Carefully manicured gardens, sliding screens, and warm natural materials: Japanese homes are refuges of tranquility, crafted in a unique domestic aesthetic of Eastern minimalism. Traditional architecture features alongside cutting-edge contemporary dwellings in this collection of homes, with many never-before-seen photographs. Turn to the rising sun and discover the fluid simplicity of these spaces where Zen philosophy breathes.

"The photographs alone are enough to keep readers entranced for hours, but tear your eyes away and the text is equally enthralling."
— *Living & Homes*, Sydney

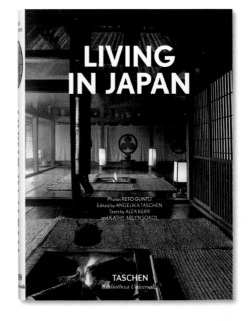

Living in Japan
Reto Guntli, Alex Kerr, Kathy Arlyn Sokol, Angelika Taschen
512 pages
TRILINGUAL EDITIONS IN:
ENGLISH / DEUTSCH / FRANÇAIS &
ESPAÑOL / ITALIANO / PORTUGUÊS

Chinese Propaganda
Posters

Film Posters of the
Russian Avant-Garde

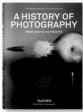

A History of
Photography

20th Century
Photography

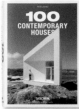

100 Contemporary
Houses

100 Interiors Around
the World

Interiors Now!

The Grand Tour

Burton Holmes.
Travelogues

Living in Japan

Living in Morocco

Living in Bali

Living in Mexico

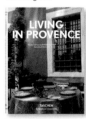

Living in Provence

Living in Tuscany

Tree Houses

Scandinavian Design

Industrial Design A-Z

domus 1950s

domus 1960s

Design of the
20th Century

1000 Chairs

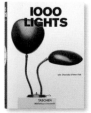

1000 Lights

Decorative Art 60s

Decorative Art 70s

100 Illustrators

Illustration Now!
Portraits

Illustration Now!
Fashion

100 Manga Artists

Logo Design

Fritz Kahn.
Infographics Pioneer

Bodoni. Manual of
Typography

The Package Design
Book

D&AD.
The Copy Book

Menu Design
in America

1000 Tattoos

Bookworm's delight:
never bore, always excite!

TASCHEN
Bibliotheca Universalis

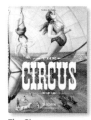
The Circus.
1870s–1950s

Mid-Century Ads

1000 Pin-Up Girls

20th Century Fashion

20th Century Travel

20th Century
Classic Cars

1000 Record Covers

Funk & Soul Covers

Jazz Covers

Extraordinary
Records

Steinweiss

L'HÔTEL PARTICULIER
ARLES

Brigitte Pagès de Oliveira's great passion is to live for interior decoration and "l'art de vivre." She installed herself in the Midi where she bought the magnificent Hôtel de Chartroux in 2001 (the former abode of the Baron de Chartroux who carried out excavations on the site of the old Roman theatre). Deciding to open the Chartroux to the public as a hotel, Brigitte sought to transform the house into a stylish 'hôtel particulier.' Working in close collaboration with the architect Paul Anouilh, she dreamt up a decor scheme that did not revolve around reconstructing the original interiors. Guests will find no trace of 18th and 19th-century French splendours nor heavy Napoleon III-style tapestries. Instead, L'Hôtel Particulier features a subtle mix of classic antique furniture and Oriental touches which include colourful Moroccan lanterns hung around the pool, a garnet-red living-room decorated with exotic paintings, and charming light-filled bedrooms furnished with sumptuous poufs and four-poster beds worthy of a pasha's palace. Grisaille wallpaper and vases from the Far East complete this perfect fusion of styles and make L'Hôtel Particulier a haven of peace and beauty.

Brigitte Pagès de Oliveiras Leidenschaft ist die Innenarchitektur und ihre liebste Kunstform heißt „l'art de vivre". Grund genug, um sich für die Hotellerie zu entscheiden und 2001 das Hôtel de Chartroux zu kaufen. Einst residierte darin ein gleichnamiger Baron, der durch die Ausgrabung eines antiken Theaters zu Ruhm und Ehren kam. Mit Hilfe des Architekten Paul Anouilh verwandelte Brigitte das Haus in ein zauberhaftes „hôtel particulier", verzichtete jedoch darauf, auch das Interieur im Stil des 18. und 19. Jahrhunderts zu gestalten. Hier gibt es weder prunkvolle Kulissen für die Hofdamen von einst noch verstaubte Draperien, sondern eine subtile Komposition klassischer Möbel mit einem Hauch von Orient. Rings um das Schwimmbecken stehen marokkanische Leuchten, und im granatroten Salon hängen exotische Bilder; die hellen Zimmer beherbergen Himmelbetten und Sitzkissen wie aus tausendundeiner Nacht, Grisaille-Tapeten und fernöstliche Vasen – Brigitte kombiniert mit leichter Hand unterschiedliche Stile und macht das Hotel zu einem Ort der Ruhe und der Schönheit.

Brigitte Pagès de Oliveira a une véritable passion pour la décoration et l'art de vivre... Voilà des bonnes raisons pour qu'elle s'éprenne de l'hôtellerie et qu'elle achète en 2001 l'Hôtel de Chartroux dans lequel habita jadis le baron du même nom, célèbre pour avoir dirigé les fouilles du théâtre antique. Transformant la maison en un charmant « hôtel particulier » avec l'aide de l'architecte Paul Anouilh, Brigitte n'a pas cherché à reconstruire les intérieurs d'époque 18e et 19e. Ici point de splendeurs dignes des belles marquises d'antan ni de lourdes tentures Napoléon III, mais un mélange subtil de meubles classiques conjugués à une touche d'orientalisme. Des lanternes marocaines autour de la piscine, un salon grenat orné de tableaux aux sujets exotiques et des chambres claires où cohabitent des lits à baldaquin, des poufs dignes du palais d'un pacha, des papiers peints style « grisaille » et des vases d'Extrême-Orient révèlent le goût de Brigitte pour le mariage des styles et font de L'Hôtel Particulier un havre de paix et de beauté.

PP. 32–33 The raised pool in the gar- den lies in the shade of the house and is surrounded by elegant recliners, para- sols and Moroccan lanterns. · Das er- höhte Schwimmbecken liegt im Schatten des Hauses. Ringsum sind Sessel, Schirme und marokkanische Laternen verteilt. · La piscine surélevée, située dans le jardin à l'ombre de la maison, est entourée de sièges, de parasols et de lanternes marocaines.

↑ A pair of terracotta lions, bearing ancient coats of arms, stand guard at the morning-room door. · Terrakottalöwen mit Wappenschilden flankieren die Türen zum kleinen Salon. · Des lions en terre cuite portant des écussons se dressent de part et d'autre de la porte du petit salon.

→ The morning room, decorated with aubergine-coloured walls, Orien-

talist paintings, baroque lamps and comfy club chairs, is a haven of peace and calm. · Gemälde mit orientalischen Motiven, auberginefarbene Wände, barocke Leuchten und bequeme Clubsessel laden die Gäste im kleinen Salon zum Verweilen ein. · Peintures orientalistes, murs couleur aubergine, luminaires baroques et fauteuils-club confortables réjouissent les hôtes qui désirent s'attarder dans le petit salon.

P. 35 The rich vermilion tones of the dining room walls provide a striking contrast to the set of white-painted country chairs. The glass-fronted cabinet at the foot of the table showcases a superb collection of decorative pottery. • Im Speisezimmer bilden die leuchtend roten Wände einen schönen Kontrast zu den weiß gestrichenen Stühlen. Der Schrank an der Rückwand beherbergt eine Sammlung dekorativer Fayencen. • Dans la salle à manger, des murs rouge vif contrastent avec des chaises rustiques

peintes en blanc. L'armoire au fond de la pièce abrite une collection de faïences décoratives.

↑ An 18th-century altar candlestick of sculptured wood has been transformed into a table lamp. • Ein ehemaliger Altarleuchter aus dem 18. Jahrhundert wurde in eine Tischlampe umgestaltet. • Un candélabre d'autel en bois sculpté d'époque dix-huitième a été transformé en lampe de table.

→ 18th-century wood panelling painted immaculate white makes the perfect backdrop for this elegant four-poster bed. The Oriental pink vase adds an agreeable touch of colour to the room. • Weiße Wandvertäfelungen aus dem 18. Jahrhundert bilden den Rahmen für das Himmelbett. Die Vase in Rosa bringt einen Hauch Farbe in den Raum. • Des boiseries 18e peintes en blanc sont l'arrière-plan idéal pour ce lit à baldaquin. Le vase oriental rose ajoute une note de couleur à la chambre.

← A pastoral grey-and-white camaieu adorns the wall of an upstairs bedroom, set off by white walls, white bed linen and a white Louis XV-style chair. • Eine ländliche Szene in Grisaille-Malerei schmückt eines der Schlafzimmer im ersten Stock. Wände, Bettwäsche und auch der Bezug des Louis-XV-Sessels sind reinweiß. • Une des chambres à l'étage a été décorée d'un camaïeu de blanc et de gris. Les murs, la literie et le revêtement de la bergère style Louis XV sont blancs.

GRAND HÔTEL
NORD-PINUS

GRAND HÔTEL NORD-PINUS
ARLES

Napoleon III was a guest in number 10, a room later occupied by a host of other celebrities including Pablo Picasso and the toreador Luis Miguel Dominguín. The photographer Lucien Clergue stayed here on trips to Arles and it was here that Helmut Newton shot his memorable portrait of the actress Charlotte Rampling. Given the colourful history of the Grand Hôtel Nord-Pinus, the original owner Anne Igou was understandably keen to step into the shoes of the famous ex-proprietress Madame Germaine. The new owner set about breathing new life into the legendary hotel in 1989, after it had lain unoccupied for 15 years. "There was absolutely nothing of the original decor left," Anne recalls, "nothing but the two boat-shaped chandeliers and the console and baroque mirror in number 10. I had to start from scratch and restore everything!" Today's guests would find it hard to imagine such a colossal undertaking. The Spanish bullfighting posters, the photographs by Lucien Clergue and Peter Lindbergh, the retro furniture and the colours seem like they have always been there.

Napoleon III. logierte in Zimmer 10, ebenso wie später Pablo Picasso, der Torero Luis Miguel Dominguín und viele andere Berühmtheiten. Zu den Gästen gehörten auch der Fotograf Lucien Clergue und Helmut Newton, der hier Charlotte Ramplings unsterbliches Porträt schuf. Als die ursprüngliche Besitzerin Anne Igou das Grand Hôtel Nord-Pinus in Arles übernahm, hatte sie deshalb allen Grund, das Werk im Geist ihrer Vorgängerin Madame Germaine fortzusetzen. Nach 15 Jahren Dornröschenschlaf hauchte sie dem legendären Hotel 1989 neues Leben ein: „Vom alten Dekor war so gut wie nichts erhalten", erinnert sich Anne. „Lediglich die beiden schiffsförmigen Kronleuchter, das Konsoltischchen und der Barockspiegel in Zimmer 10 waren noch vorhanden. Alles musste ich erneuern, alles restaurieren!" Wer heute im Nord-Pinus absteigt, kann sich kaum noch vorstellen, was für eine Sisyphusarbeit dahintersteckt. Die spanischen Stierkampfplakate, die Farben, die Fotos von Lucien Clergue und Peter Lindbergh und das nostalgische Mobiliar wirken durch und durch original.

Napoléon III y occupa la chambre 10, précédant Pablo Picasso, le toréador Luis Miguel Dominguín et bien d'autres célébrités. Le photographe Lucien Clergue y a séjourné et Helmut Newton y a réalisé l'inoubliable portrait de l'actrice Charlotte Rampling. L'ancienne propriétaire Anne Igou avait donc de bonnes raisons de reprendre le flambeau de la fameuse ex-directrice Madame Germaine en devenant à son tour propriétaire du Grand Hôtel Nord-Pinus à Arles. Elle a redonné vie en 1989 à cet endroit légendaire qui avait été inoccupé pendant 15 ans. « Il ne restait plus rien de l'ancien décor », se souvient Anne - « juste les deux lustres en forme de bateau et la console et le miroir baroque dans la 10. J'ai dû tout refaire. Tout restaurer ! » Aujourd'hui les hôtes du Nord-Pinus ne peuvent guère s'imaginer les travaux de Sisyphe qui ont été entrepris à l'époque. Les affiches de tauromachie espagnoles, les couleurs, les photographies de Lucien Clergue et de Peter Lindbergh et le mobilier rétro donnent l'impression d'avoir toujours été là.

PP. 42–43 The monumental staircase is adorned with a Louis XV banister in elegant wrought iron and hung with antique posters. • Das weitläufige Treppenhaus mit dem schmiedeeisernen Louis-XV-Geländer und alten Plakaten. • La vaste cage d'escalier avec sa rampe en fer forgé Louis XV et ses anciennes affiches.

P. 45 Embroidered gauze curtains flutter in the summer breeze, bathing the restaurant in a soft glow. • Durchscheinende, bestickte Gardinen lassen sanftes Licht ins Restaurant und bewegen sich in der Sommerbrise. • Des rideaux diaphanes brodés tamisent la lumière qui baigne la salle de restaurant et flottent dans une brise d'été.

↑ A statue of Frédéric Mistral stands proudly in the Place du Forum, observing the hustle and bustle of tourists trying to find a seat on the café terraces below. • Das stolze Standbild Frédéric Mistrals dominiert die Place du Forum und schaut auf die Touristen herab, die sich auf den zahlreichen Caféterrassen tummeln. • La fière statue de Frédéric Mistral semble dominer la place du Forum et regarder les touristes qui essayent de trouver un siège à la terrasse d'un des nombreux cafés.

→ The legendary façade of the Nord-Pinus. Behind the balcony, which runs the entire length of the building, is the famous toreadors' suite. • Die berühmte Fassade des Nord-Pinus. Hinter dem Balkon, der über die ganze Breite verläuft, liegt das „Torero-Zimmer". • La célèbre façade du Nord-Pinus. Derrière le balcon tout en longueur se trouve la fameuse chambre des toréadors.

↑ The convivial decor in the bar conjures up images of an old-fashioned bistro from a Marcel Pagnol novel. · Die Dekoration der Bar erinnert an gemütliche Bistros wie bei Marcel Pagnol. · La décoration du bar évoque l'ambiance conviviale des bistros à la Marcel Pagnol.

→ Anne Igou's rich red colour scheme made a stunning backdrop for these photographs of famous bullfighters. · Für die Wände wählte Anne Igou Rot, das die schönen Fotos berühmter Stierkämpfer hervorhebt. · Anne Igou avait choisi des murs rouges pour exalter la beauté des photographies de toréadors célèbres.

← Napoleon III and Picasso both slept in the famous toreadors' suite. The baroque console and mirror made a stunning backdrop for Charlotte Rampling when she posed for photographer Helmut Newton. • Napoleon III. und Picasso übernachteten im „Torero-Zimmer". Barockkonsole und -spiegel dienten schon als Hintergrund für Helmut Newtons berühmtes Porträt von Charlotte Rampling. • Napoléon III et Picasso ont dormi dans la chambre des toréadors. La console et le miroir baroque ont aussi servi de décor à Charlotte Rampling quand elle a posé pour Helmut Newton.

↑ Many celebrities have slept in this magnificent upstairs bedroom. • In diesem Bett in einem der Schlafzimmer haben schon unzählige Berühmtheiten genächtigt. • Dans une chambre à l'étage, ce lit splendide a accueilli nombre de célébrités.

LE CLOÎTRE
ARLES

Le Cloître is not only centrally located in Arles, in a peaceful part of town; it is also uniquely beautiful in its decor. The Swiss patron of the arts Maja Hoffmann, who owns the hotel, commissioned the Franco-Lebanese architect India Mahdavi to carry out the renovation and furnishing of the historic building. Hand-stitched linen and velvet curtains, custom-made furniture such as sofas, wardrobes and room dividers in combination with selected pieces of furniture by the Bouroullec brothers, Gio Ponti, and the workshops of Vittorio Bonacina adorn the rooms, with their flood of sunlight. The special light of Arles had already lured Vincent van Gogh and Paul Gauguin into the town, which nowadays is famous for its annual Festival of Contemporary Photography. The decisive colour design in Le Cloître reminds one very pleasantly of this marriage of light and creativity. Then there is the location of the house: from the roof terrace, the view extends over the Saint Trophime cathedral to the Roman theatre.

Das Le Cloître ist nicht nur zentral, zugleich aber sehr ruhig in Arles gelegen, sondern auch einmalig schön eingerichtet. Die Schweizer Kunstmäzenin Maja Hoffmann, der das Hotel gehört, hat die französisch-libanesische Architektin India Mahdavi mit dem Umbau und der Einrichtung des historischen Gebäudes beauftragt. Handgenähte Vorhänge aus Leinen und Samt, maßgefertigte Möbel wie Sofas, Schränke und Raumteiler in Kombination mit ausgewählten Möbelstücken der Gebrüder Bouroullec, Gio Ponti sowie aus den Werkstätten von Vittorio Bonacina zieren die sonnendurchfluteten Räume. Das spezielle Licht in Arles hat schon Vincent van Gogh und Paul Gauguin in das Städtchen gelockt, das heute vor allem für das alljährliche Festival der modernen Fotografie berühmt ist. Die entschiedene Farbgestaltung im Le Cloître erinnert auf schöne Weise an die Vermählung von Licht und Schaffenslust. Hinzu kommt die Lage des Hauses: Von der Dachterrasse aus schweift der Blick über die Kathedrale Saint Trophime bis zum römischen Theater.

Le Cloître à Arles est central, mais aussi très tranquille, et surtout aménagé avec un goût unique. La mécène suisse Maja Hoffmann, propriétaire de l'hôtel, a confié la transformation et l'installation du bâtiment historique à l'architecte franco-libanaise India Mahdavi. Des rideaux de lin et velours cousus main, du mobilier sur mesure tel que canapés, armoires et meubles de séparation, associés à d'autres sélectionnés des frères Bouroullec, de Gio Ponti ou des ateliers de Vittorio Bonacina, ornent les pièces baignées de soleil. La lumière propre à Arles a déjà attiré Vincent van Gogh et Paul Gauguin dans la petite ville, aujourd'hui plus célèbre pour son festival annuel de photographie. Le choix résolu des couleurs du Cloître rappelle en beauté ce mariage de la lumière et du désir créateur. Il faut y ajouter la situation : depuis le toit en terrasse, le regard erre de la cathédrale Saint Trophime au théâtre antique.

PP. 52–53 The hotel façade has remained intact and possesses the irresistible charm of the old Provençal houses. Settling down on the terrace under the shade of the 100-year-old paulownia tree, we feel we're in a dream. • Die historische Fassade des Hauses ist intakt und strahlt den unwiderstehlichen Charme traditioneller provenzalischer Architektur aus. Unter einem hundertjährigen Blauglockenbaum auf der Terrasse lässt es sich gut aushalten. • La façade de l'hôtel est restée intacte et elle possède le charme irrésistible des vieilles demeures de Provence. Il est doux de s'installer sur la terrasse et de s'abriter à l'ombre d'un Paulownia centenaire.

P. 55 The blue colourwashed walls lend a fresh note to the stairwell. • Die blau gekalkten Wände geben dem Treppenhaus eine angenehme Kühle. • Des murs badigeonnés en bleu donnent une note de fraîcheur à la cage d'escalier.

→ India Mahdavi has succeeded in marrying rustical and contemporary styles. The shelves, with their colourfully painted bottles, bring a touch of gaiety. • India Mahdavi hat hier wunderbar rustikales und zeitgenössisches Design zusammengebracht. Durch die bunten Farben geben die Flaschen dem Raum eine beschwingte Note. • India Mahdavi a réussi à marier le rustique et le contemporain. L'étagère aux bouteilles peintes en couleurs vives apporte une touche de gaieté.

P. 58 The granite-covered floor is coated with a marble resin. Its arabesques imitate the line of a carpet edge. • Auf dem Granit-Boden bilden Arabesken aus marmoriertem Kunstharz ein Teppichmuster. • Le sol recouvert de Granito a été incrusté avec une résine en marbre dont les arabesques imitent le dessin d'un tapis.

P. 59 Beyond a door, a Mahdavi sofa and various contemporary paintings form an ensemble of striking colours. • Die geöffnete Tür gibt den Blick frei auf ein Sofa von Mahdavi, das zusammen mit den zeitgenössischen Gemälden ein Ensemble in strahlenden Farben ergibt. • Au-delà d'une porte, un canapé signé Mahdavi et des tableaux d'artistes contemporains forment un ensemble aux couleurs éclatantes.

↑ In this room, the famous designer has given the background wall an astonishing mural which doubles as a headboard. The "Cap Martin" rattan furniture also carries her signature and is inspired by an original model from the 1950s. • In diesem Zimmer hat die namhafte Designerin eine große Wandmalerei angebracht, die gleichzeitig das Kopfteil des Bettes ersetzt. Die Rattanmöbel aus ihrer Serie „Cap Martin" sind von einem Original-Entwurf aus den 1950er-

Jahren beeinflusst. • Dans cette chambre la célèbre créatrice a doté le mur de fond avec une décoration murale étonnante qui fait également office de tête de lit. Le mobilier en rotin baptisé « Cap Martin » porte également sa signature et s'inspire d'un modèle original des années 1950.

→ The choice of furniture and colours nostalgically harks back to the 1950s, but in Mahdavi's hands the final result is strictly contemporary. • Die Auswahl der Möbel und das Farbkonzept sind von den Fünfzigern angeregt, aber die Designerin hat dem Ganzen eine entschieden zeitgenössische Note gegeben. • Le choix des meubles et des couleurs est un clin d'œil au style « fifties », mais grâce à Mahdavi le résultat final est résolument contemporain.

↑ In the bathroom the guest will discover an original washbasin from the
"Bishop" line created by Mahdavi. ·
In einem Badezimmer entdeckt man
ein originelles Waschbecken aus der Serie „Bishop" von Mahdavi. · Dans une
salle de bains, on découvre un lavabo
à la forme originale qui fait partie de la
ligne « Bishop » crée par Mahdavi.

→ In this bathroom you have the impression that the floor of "crazy" marble
tiles is climbing up the back wall and
spattering it with a unique mosaic. ·
Hier hat man den Eindruck, dass die
unregelmäßig gearbeiteten Boden-
platten aus Marmor die Wände des
Badezimmers hinaufklettern, um sie
mit einem einzigartigen Mosaik zu

bedecken. · Dans cette salle de bains
on a l'impression que le sol en dalles
de marbre irrégulières grimpe le long
des murs en éclaboussant le bas d'une
mosaïque singulière.

LA MIRANDE

LA MIRANDE
STEIN FAMILY
AVIGNON

More than 20 years ago La Mirande, the stylish 'hôtel particulier' which stands in a tranquil cobbled square at the foot of the Palais des Papes in Avignon, opened its imposing doors embellished with grotesque masks. Since then, guests from all over the world have stayed in this magnificent residence, tastefully restored and decorated by the Stein family. Expressing their passion for the decorative arts and architecture of the 18th century, Achim and Hannelore Stein and their son, Martin, worked in close collaboration with the interior decorator François Joseph Graff. The Steins sought to make their restoration of the former Hôtel Pamard as authentic as possible and, at the same time, create a warm and welcoming atmosphere. The family wanted guests to feel as if they were staying in the home of an old family from the Provençal aristocracy. The luxuriously comfortable interiors feature period furniture, wood panelling, floral wallpaper, beautiful engravings and rustic pieces of earthenware. Needless to say, La Mirande has established a reputation as one of the most upmarket destinations in Avignon.

Über 20 Jahre ist es schon her, seit La Mirande seine mit skurrilen Masken verzierten Pforten öffnete. Seither haben Gäste aus aller Welt das Hotel zu Füßen des Papstpalastes in Avignon besucht, das mit so viel Liebe zum Detail und Begeisterung für die Architektur und das Kunsthandwerk des 18. Jahrhunderts neu gestaltet wurde. Um den Stil möglichst authentisch nachzubilden, ließen sich Achim, Hannelore und Martin Stein bei der Restaurierung des ehemaligen Hôtel Pamard von dem Innenarchitekten François Joseph Graff beraten. Am Herzen lag ihnen vor allem, dem vornehmen Stadthaus eine warme, einladende Atmosphäre zu verleihen. Da die Steins selbst für die Provence schwärmen, wollten sie auch ihren Gästen das Gefühl vermitteln, bei einer alten provenzalischen Adelsfamilie zu Gast zu sein: Die komfortablen Zimmer sind mit Stilmöbeln, Holzvertäfelungen und romantischen Tapeten ausgestattet, ergänzt durch gemusterte Indienne-Stoffe, Stiche und rustikale Fayencen. La Mirande gehört zu Recht zu den ersten Häusern Avignons, wenn nicht sogar der Welt.

Plus de 20 ans déjà que La Mirande a ouvert ses portes imposantes ornées de mascarons au pied du Palais des Papes à Avignon. Depuis, des hôtes du monde entier ont séjourné dans ce bel hôtel particulier restauré et décoré par la famille Stein avec un goût et un souci du détail qui révèlent leur passion pour l'architecture et les arts décoratifs du 18e siècle. Guidés dans leur recherche de l'authenticité par le décorateur François Joseph Graff, Achim et Hannelore Stein et leur fils Martin ont restauré l'ancien Hôtel Pamard avec l'intention d'y créer une ambiance chaleureuse et accueillante. Amoureux de la Provence, ils désiraient que leurs hôtes aient l'impression de séjourner chez une de ces vieilles familles de l'aristocratie provençale, dans un intérieur confortable, entourés de meubles d'époque, de lambris et de papiers peints fleuris, le tout enjolivé par la présence d'indiennes, de gravures et de belles faïences rustiques. La Mirande, faut-il s'en étonner, est devenue un haut lieu d'Avignon et une révélation dans le monde hôtelier.

PP. 64–65 Time has stopped in the enclosed garden of La Mirande and guests have the privilege of dining al fresco amid luxuriant greenery. • Im von Mauern umschlossenen Garten des La Mirande scheint die Zeit stehen geblieben zu sein, und die Gäste können die Mahlzeiten im Freien inmitten einer prächtig blühenden Vegetation einnehmen. Welch ein Privileg! • Le temps s'est arrêté dans le jardin clos de murs de la Mirande et les hôtes ont le privilège de pouvoir prendre leurs repas « al fresco » parmi une végétation luxuriante.

P. 67 The imposing door of the former Hôtel Pamard is decorated with a pair of Baroque mascarons. The bronze lion-head door knockers are typical of the doors of the grand residences of Avignon. • Die monumentale Tür des

ehemaligen Hôtel Pamard ist mit zwei barocken Mascarons geschmückt. Darunter bronzene Löwenköpfe mit Türklopfern, wie man sie an vielen Herrenhäusern der Region findet. • La porte monumentale de l'ancien Hôtel Pamard s'orne d'une paire de « mascherones » broques. Les heurtoirs en bronze en forme de tête de lion sont typiques pour les portes des grandes demeures Avignonnaises.

↑ The same attention to period detail is evident in the reception room. This terracotta statuette of a shepherdess from 1900 is set off against wood panelling in Louis XVI style. • Auch der Empfangssalon ist mit viel Liebe zum historischen Detail gestaltet. Das bukolische Tonfigürchen aus der Zeit um 1900 harmoniert perfekt mit der Vertäfelung im Louis-

XVI-Stil. • Le même soin du détail d'époque se reflète dans le salon. Une statuette de bergère d'époque 1900 en terre cuite se marie avec des boiseries dans le style Louis XVI.

→ The door of La Mirande opens onto an entrance hall and a covered courtyard that offers an oasis to anyone who wants to relax over afternoon tea or an aperitif. • Durch das Tor des La Mirande tretend, gelangt man durch den Eingangsraum zu einem überdachten Hof, der den Besuchern zur Stunde des „afternoon tea" oder Aperitifs einen Ort der Entspannung bietet. • La porte de La Mirande s'ouvre sur une entrée et une cour couverte qui offre le refuge à ceux qui veulent s'y détendre à l'heure du thé ou plus tard de l'apéritif.

↑ La Mirande features the most sumptuous design details. The restaurant is hung with a 17th-century Flemish tapestry. · La Mirande steht auch für prächtiges Dekor. So hängt im Restaurant ein flämischer Wandteppich aus dem 17. Jahrhundert. · La Mirande abonde aussi de détails somptueux:

dans la salle de restaurant une tapisserie flamande du 17ᵉ.

→ From the covered courtyard, guests can enter the restaurant. The serving table is no longer noticeable under an embroidered tablecloth of the Napoleon III period. · Vom überdachten Hof

aus kann man sich direkt ins Speisezimmer begeben. Den Beistelltisch bedeckt eine besticktes Tischtuch aus der Zeit Napoleons III. · De la cour couverte les hôtes peuvent se rendre directement dans la salle du restaurant. La table de service disparaît sous une nappe brodée d'époque Napoléon III.

PP. 72–73 In the restaurant dining room, an impressive collection of storage jars and varnished earthenware Provençal jugs has a place of honour on a former draper's table. • Das Speisezimmer ziert eine Sammlung von Tongefäßen aus der Provence. Hübsch präsentieren sie sich auf einem ehemaligen Schneiderei-Tisch. • Dans la salle à manger du restaurant une collection impressionnante de jarres et de cruches provençales en terre cuite vernissée a trouvé une place d'honneur sur une ancienne table de drapier.

↑ In the rustic kitchen in the basement, this massive beechwood table is set for a Provençal feast. • In der Küche im Souterrain genießen die Gäste an einem langen Buchentisch provenzalische Köstlichkeiten. • Dans la cuisine du sous-sol, la grande table en hêtre attend ceux qui se laisseront séduire par la cuisine provençale.

→ Every Friday, Martin Stein hosts a dinner which pays rich homage to the local cuisine. Here, the renowned chef prepares a delicious Provençal dish. •

Freitags lädt Martin Stein zu einem Gastessen, das eine echte Liebeserklärung an die provenzalische Küche ist. Das Gericht, das der renommierte Küchenchef hier zubereitet, verströmt die delikaten Aromen dieser einmaligen Landschaft. • Tous les vendredis, Martin Stein préside une table d'hôte qui est un véritable hommage à la cuisine provençale. Ici, le chef renommé prépare un plat délicieux aux arômes de Provence.

PP. 76–77 In the cosy living room, set aside for intimate dinners, a huge glass-fronted cupboard displays a stunning collection of 18th-century crockery. • In dem für kleine Tischgesellschaften reservierten Salon steht ein wunderschönes Service aus dem 18. Jahrhundert in einer Vitrine. • Dans le salon destiné aux dîners intimes, une armoire vitrée de dimensions généreuses abrite une splendide vaisselle 18e.

↑ A majestic stone staircase adorned with a Louis XV cold-welded wrought iron rail leads to the upper storeys. • Eine stattliche Treppe führt die Besucher in die oberen Geschosse. Beachtenswert auch das Eisengeländer aus der Zeit Louis XV, hergestellt im Kaltschmiede-Verfahren. • Un majestueux escalier en pierre agrémenté d'une rampe d'époque Louis XV en fer forgé – soudée à froid – mène vers les étages.

→ This narrow corridor, leading to one of the bathrooms, is decorated with a rustic chair and an 18th-century engraving set off against the floral wallpaper. • Ein rustikaler Stuhl und ein Stich aus dem 18. Jahrhundert auf farbenfroher Tapete leiten im Korridor zu einem der Bäder. • Dans un passage étroit qui mène vers une salle de bains, une chaise rustique et une gravure 18e sur fond de papier peint.

↑ The Steins love hunting for antique bargains. All over the hotel you will come across their delightful finds. · Die Familie Stein stöbert gern nach schönen alten Dingen, und überall im Hotel kann man glückliche Funde bestaunen. · Les Stein sont des « chineurs » d'antiquités passionnés et partout dans l'hôtel on découvre leurs trouvailles hereuses.

→ In the little drawing room that looks directly over the garden, the 18th-century wallpaper is hand-painted with chinoiseries. An elegant sofa in the Directoire style invites the guest to relax. · Vom kleinen Salon aus erreicht man schnell den Garten. Die Wände sind mit Tapeten aus dem 18. Jahrhundert verziert, handbemalt mit Chinoisierien. ·

Dans le petit salon qui donne directement sur le jardin, les parois s'habillent d'un papier peint d'époque 18e décoré à la main avec des « chinoiseries ». Un élégant canapé de style Directoire invite à la détente.

↑ One word sums up La Mirande: perfection – and the hotel staff are synonymous with impeccable service. • „Perfektion" ist das Wort, mit dem sich das La Mirande am besten charakterisieren lässt, und das Personal kümmert sich um die Gäste mit einwandfreiem

Service. • Qui dit La Mirande dit « perfection » et le personnel de l'hôtel est synonyme d'un service impeccable.

→ This Empire-style panel in one of the bedrooms was inspired by the treasures of Roman antiquity and excavations at

Pompeii. • Die klassizistischen Bildtapeten in einem der Zimmer haben altrömische Motive und Wandmalereien aus Pompeji zum Vorbild. • Une des chambres a été tendue de panneaux de style Empire inspirés par les fouilles de Pompéi et par l'antiquité romaine.

← The rooms have been decorated in the purest 18th-century style, and guests will naturally discover Jouy textiles, wallpaper by Mauny and old engravings. • Alle Zimmer sind im Stil des 18. Jahrhunderts eingerichtet, und so findet man hier Toile-de-Jouy-Stoffe, Tapeten von Mauny und historische Stiche. • Les chambres ont été décorées dans le plus pur style 18ᵉ et on y découvre d'office des Toiles de Jouy, des papiers peints édités par Mauny et des gravures anciennes.

↑ For the curtains and the armchair upholstery, the Steins opted for Braquenié/Pierre Frey fabrics that have been recreated from contemporary documents. •

Für Vorhänge und Sesselbezüge hat das Ehepaar Stein Textilien der Firma Braquenié/Pierre Frey ausgesucht. Es sind Wiederauflagen historischer Stoffe. • Pour les rideaux et le recouvrement des fauteuils, les Stein ont opté pour des tissus de chez Braquenié/Pierre Frey qui sont des rééditions de documents d'époque.

↑ Indienne textiles are often decorated with a pattern called "arbre de vie" (tree of life), and this certainly creates the mood of this suite. • Die Textilien der Serie „Indienne" sind häufig mit dem Motiv des Lebensbaums versehen, und in dieser Suite ist er allgegenwärtig. • Les tissus de type « Indienne » sont souvent décorés avec un dessin nommé « arbre de vie » et dans cette suite sa présence domine la décoration.

→ The windows of one of the bathrooms open up to allow a wide view of the terrace and hotel garden. • Ein wunderbarer Ausblick auf Terrasse und Garten des Hotels durch die großen Fenster des Badezimmers. • Les fenêtres d'une des salles de bain s'ouvrent grand sur la terrasse et le jardin de l'hôtel.

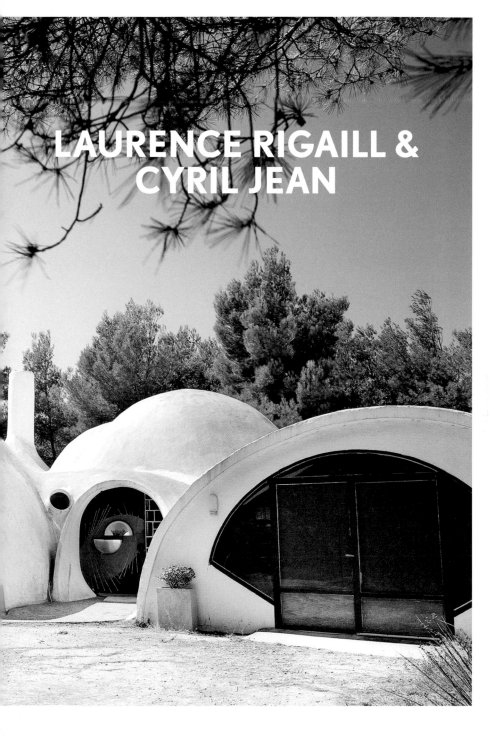

LAURENCE RIGAILL &
CYRIL JEAN

LAURENCE RIGAILL
& CYRIL JEAN

AVIGNON

One of a series of "Bubble Houses" built near Avignon, whose organic curves provide womb-like security. The cave-like interiors are ideal for a collection of 1960s design, especially oriented towards the Space Age.

Eines der berühmten „Bubble Houses" in der Nähe von Avignon, deren organische Rundungen für eine Geborgenheit wie im Mutterleib sorgen sollen. Die höhlenartigen Räume sind ideal für eine Sammlung von Designobjekten aus den 1960ern.

Une des « maisons bulles » construites près d'Avignon et dont les formes organiques visent à recréer l'utérus protecteur. Ses intérieurs, évoquant des grottes, sont idéaux pour accueillir une collection de design des années 1960 particulièrement influencé par l'ère spatiale.

PP. 88–89 The cement forms of the house were apparently inspired by an imaginary prehistoric creature. · Die Zementformen des Hauses sind offenbar von einem imaginären prähistorischen Wesen inspiriert. · Les formes en ciment de la maison s'inspireraient d'une créature préhistorique imaginaire.

P. 91 A "Panton" chair by the doorway leading into the indoor garden. · Ein „Panton"-Stuhl neben dem Durchgang zum Innengarten. · Un siège « Panton » près de la porte donnant sur le jardin d'hiver.

← Teak stepping stones and a suspended wicker chair in the indoor garden. · Trittsteine aus Teak und ein hängender Korbsessel im Innengarten. · Des marches en teck descendent dans le jardin d'hiver où un fauteuil en rotin est suspendu.

↑ In the guestoom, a concrete platform for a single bed is suspended from the ceiling. The lamp to the right dates from the late 1960s. · Im Gästezimmer wurde eine Betonzwischendecke als Schlafstätte von der Decke abgehängt. Die Lampe rechts stammt aus den 1960ern. · Dans la chambre d'amis,

une plaque en béton en guise de lit est suspendue au plafond. La lampe sur la droite date des années 1960.

PP. 94–95 In the main living area are two Eero Aarnio chairs dating from 1967. Stools provide seating at the wenge-stained laminate kitchen counter. · Zwei Stühle von Eero Aarnio von 1967 im großen Wohnbereich. An der Küchentheke aus gebeizter Wenge kann man auf Hockern Platz nehmen. · Dans le séjour principal, deux fauteuils d'Eero Aarnio datant de 1967. Des tabourets entourent le comptoir de cuisine en stratifié teinté en palissandre d'Afrique.

↑ An Eero Aarnio "Ball Chair" stands on a round carpet. The dining table and chairs are from Eero Saarinen's iconic "Tulip" series. • Ein „Ball Chair" von Eero Aarnio auf einem runden Teppich. Der Esstisch und die Stühle gehören zu Eero Saarinens legendären „Tulip"-Entwürfen. • Un « Fauteuil ballon » d'Eero Aarnio posé sur un tapis rond. La table et les chaises de la salle à manger appartiennent à la célèbre ligne « Tulip » d'Eero Saarinen.

→ Inside, one space flows into the next. The small table to the right is Emma Gismondi Schweinberger's "Giano Vano". • Innen geht ein Raum in den nächsten über. Der kleine Tisch rechts ist das Modell „Giano Vano" von Emma Gismondi Schweinberger. • Les espaces s'enchaînent. Sur la droite, un petit guéridon « Giano Vano » d'Emma Gismondi Schweinberger.

↓ An eye-shaped window provides both a niche for relaxing and a view into the indoor garden. • Das wie ein Auge geformte Fenster bietet sowohl eine Nische zum Entspannen als auch einen Blick in den Innengarten. • Une ouverture en forme d'œil offre à la fois un recoin pour se détendre et une vue sur le jardin d'hiver.

→ The "Bubble Salon" is decorated with a semi-circular banquette and a white cement fireplace. • Der „Bubble Salon" ist mit einer halbkreisförmigen gepolsterten Sitzbank und einem weißen Kamin aus Zement ausgestattet. • Dans le « salon bulle », une banquette en demi-cercle et une cheminée blanche en plâtre.

MICHELLE & YVES
HALARD

MICHELLE & YVES HALARD
LE THOR

"I loathe decoration!" Michelle declares. Throughout her long and successful career as an interior decorator and designer of textiles, household linens, lamps and tableware, this remarkable woman has defended the anti-decor movement to the hilt, promoting a return to the simple values of the family home. "I'm totally disorganised," Michelle insists, although her designs utterly refute her claims, and the interiors she created with her late husband, Yves, exude a calm sense of spontaneity and well-being. The Halards claim to have lived in Paris "for ever," but they had never given up on the idea of finding a second home in Provence. Leaving their magnificent 'château' in the Berry region, the couple set off on a quest of the South. And a long and eventful quest it turned out to be, as they trawled through "all those renovated houses and modern bathrooms tiled with daisy motifs that didn't appeal to us at all." One day, the Halards came across a dilapidated 18th-century farmhouse which let them exercise their talent for transforming a rustic ruin into a charming home, filled with a delightful assortment of furniture, treasured objects and family souvenirs arranged with the couple's orderly nonchalance.

„Ich hasse Dekorationen!", verkündet Michelle, und es stimmt: Während ihrer Laufbahn als Innenarchitektin und Designerin von Stoffen und Lampen, von Bett- und Tischwäsche bis hin zu Tafelgeschirr hat sie stets vehement die Vorzüge der „Anti-Dekoration" verteidigt. Ihr Ideal ist das gemütliche Zuhause. „Ich bin sehr unordentlich", behauptet diese bemerkenswerte Frau, doch ihre Kreationen beweisen das Gegenteil. Die gemeinsam mit ihrem mittlerweile verstorbenen Ehemann Yves gestalteten Interieurs zeichnen sich durch Spontaneität und Behaglichkeit aus. Beide wohnten zwar „immer schon" in Paris, träumten jedoch ebenso lange von einem zweiten Wohnsitz in der Provence. Von ihrem Schloss im Berry aus eroberten sie Südfrankreich. Die rastlose Suche war zunächst eher enttäuschend: „All die renovierten Häuser und modernen Bäder mit ihren Blümchenfliesen überzeugten uns nicht im Geringsten." Das tat erst ein großes, halb verfallenes Bauernhaus aus dem 18. Jahrhundert; es bot den Halards Gelegenheit, erneut ihr einzigartiges Talent zu beweisen: Aus einer Ruine machten sie ein Haus voller bunt zusammengewürfelter Möbel, charmanter Accessoires und Andenken, das die für sie typische Atmosphäre wohl geordneter Lässigkeit verströmt.

« Je déteste la décoration ! » s'exclame Michelle. De fait, tout au long de sa carrière de décoratrice et de créatrice de tissus, de lampes, de linge de maison et de services de table, personne n'a mieux défendu les bienfaits de l'anti-décoration et de la maison de famille, chaleureuse et accueillante. « Je suis désordonnée » ajoute cette femme remarquable dont les réalisations démentent ces propos et qui a signé avec son feu mari, Yves, des intérieurs marqués par la spontanéité et le sens du bien-être. Installés à Paris « depuis toujours », les Halard n'avaient jamais abandonné l'idée d'une seconde résidence en Provence. Ils ont quitté leur magnifique château du Berry pour partir à la conquête du Midi. Conquête mouvementée et déprimante car « toutes les maisons rénovées et toutes ces salles de bains modernes décorées avec des carrelages aux motif de pâquerettes n'avaient rien pour nous plaire ». En revanche une grande maison de cultivateurs 18ᵉ, en très mauvais état, leur a permis de prouver à nouveau leur don unique de transformer une ruine en une maison remplie de meubles hétéroclites, d'objets charmants et de souvenirs de famille et où règne une nonchalance ordonnée caractéristique.

PP. 100–101 The large farmhouse has been transformed into a Provençal villa, and the terrace, decorated with a profusion of plants and delightful garden furniture, expresses Michelle's innate flair. • Aus dem ehemaligen Weingut ist eine provenzalische Villa geworden. Auf der üppig begrünten Terrasse zeugen die hinreißenden Gartenmöbel von Michelles beherztem Willen zum Stil-Mix. • La grande maison de cultivateur a été transformée en villa provençale et la terrasse décorée avec une profusion de plantes et un ravissant mobilier de jardin témoigne du « panache » de Michelle.

← and P. 103 Michelle Halard knows how to preserve her houses intact. This one is imposing but has rustic charm. Despite new colourwash on the walls and a fresh coat of paint on the shutters, the house retains its original soul. • Bei allem Glanz ist das Haus durchaus rustikal, denn Michelle Halard belässt alte Häuser intakt. Auch ein frischer Anstrich und neu lackierte Fensterläden nehmen Michelles Heim nichts vom Charme vergangener Tage. • La maison est à la fois grandiose et rustique. Et Michelle Halard sait laisser ses maisons intactes. En dépit d'un nouveau badigeon et des volets repeints, la demeure a gardé son charme d'antan.

↑ The house has retained its period wrought ironwork and the Halards have kept to a subdued 18th-century colour scheme, keeping the house as close as possible to its original hues. • Das Haus besitzt noch die alten Fenstergitter. Bei der Farbwahl entschieden sich die Halards für zarte Töne, die den ursprünglichen Nuancen nachempfunden sind. • La maison a conservé ses ferronneries d'époque. Et côté couleur, les Halard ont choisi une délicate palette 18ᵉ qui se rapproche des teintes originales.

↑ The legendary couple seated in front of the house. The outsize garden bench has been painted a lively blue. • Das legendäre Ehepaar vor seiner Villa. Die überdimensionale Gartenbank ist in strahlendem Blau gehalten. • Le couple mythique assis devant la maison. Le banc de jardin aux proportions démesurées a été peint en bleu vif.

→ Michelle has arranged a set of classic garden furniture in front of the house. The tablecloth is an ingenious reinvention of an old linen bedsheet dyed eye-catching pink. • Vor dem Haus hat Michelle klassische Gartenmöbel aufgestellt. Als Tischdecke dient ein schönes altes Betttuch in leuchtendem Rosa. • Michelle a installé devant sa maison des meubles de jardin classiques. La nappe n'est autre qu'un drap de lit ancien teint en rose vif.

PP. 108 and 109 An 18th-century staircase and tiled floor. The Halards did not alter the house's original architecture or period features. • Bodenfliesen und Treppe aus dem 18. Jahrhundert wurden wie auch die Architektur und zeitgenössische Details von den Halards nicht angetastet. • Sol à dallages et cage d'escalier 18e: les Halard n'ont pas touché à l'architecture et aux détails d'époque.

↑ Michelle's original creations are scattered all over the house. One also finds them on a simple garden table set for an afternoon snack. · Michelles Original-Entwürfe sind überall im Haus zu finden, hier zum Beispiel auf einem einfachen Gartentisch, der für einen kleinen Imbiss am Nachmittag gedeckt ist. · Les créations originales de Michelle sont partout dans la maison et on les retrouve aussi sur une simple table de jardin, dressée à l'occasion pour un goûter.

→ In the little dining room, wrought-iron garden chairs dating from the 1940s also have a place at the table. Their unusual presence is perfectly adapted to the old furniture and decor of the period. · Im kleinen Speisesaal finden sich schmiedeeiserne Gartenstühle im Stil der 1940er-Jahre. Sie umgeben einen altertümlichen Esstisch und fügen sich fabelhaft ins historische Dekor. · Dans la petite salle à manger des chaises de jardin en fer forgé « années 1940 » ont trouvé une place autour de la table et leur présence inhabituelle s'adapte parfaitement au mobilier ancien et au décor d'époque.

PP. 112–113 The sunflower-yellow living room is furnished with sumptuous Napoleon III armchairs, antique chairs, designer stools and quirky garden gnomes designed by Philippe Starck. The look is totally "Halard", yet totally Provence. · Im sonnengelben Wohnraum stehen Polstersessel im Stil Napoleons III. und schöne alte Stühle neben Designerhockern und den kecken Gartenzwergen von Philippe Starck. Der Effekt ist „typisch Halard" und doch provenzalisch. · Le séjour jaune tournesol abrite des fauteuils capitonnés Napoléon III, des chaises de style, des tabourets design et de charmants gnomes signés Philippe Starck. Le résultat est indéniablement « Halard » et indiscutablement provençal.

← Michelle works on her fabric samples like a painter in front of an easel. She's always searching for glowing colours and shimmering materials for her next collections. • Auf der Suche nach neuen schillernden Kombinationen arbeitet Michelle wie ein Maler vor seiner Staffelei. Farben und Stoffe für ihre neue Kollektion finden hier zum ersten Mal zusammen. • Michelle travaille à ses échantillons de tissus comme un peintre travaille devant son chevalet et elle s'efforce à chaque fois de trouver des couleurs et des matériaux chatoyants qui formeront ses prochaines collections.

↑ At the Halard home, everything and anything can offer potential for the designer. Today this old painter's palette will be the source of inspiration for the fabrics of tomorrow. • Bei den Eheleuten Halard dient alles der Kreativität, und hier bietet eine alte Malerpalette die Inspiration für zukünftige Textilien. • Chez les Halard tout est propice à la création et aujourd'hui l'ancienne palette d'un peintre va inspirer les tissus de demain.

PP. 116–117 The library is much more than a haven for an impressive collection of books and documents; at the same time it is a source of information and inspiration. • Die Bibliothek beherbergt eine beeindruckende Sammlung von Büchern und Dokumenten. Sie ist nicht nur ein Rückzugsort, sondern auch eine Quelle des Wissens und der Inspiration. • La bibliothèque est beaucoup plus qu'un refuge pour une impressionnante collection de livres et de documents car elle est à la fois une source d'information et une source d'inspiration.

↑ In one of the rooms, a bed with a duchess-style canopy has been covered by Michelle in an exotically-patterned toile de Jouy fabric. • In einem Zimmer ein Himmelbett „a la duchesse" – einer Herzogin würdig – bedeckt von antikem Toile-de-Jouy-Stoff mit exotischen Motiven. • Dans une des chambres un lit avec un baldaquin « à la duchesse » a été habillé par Michelle avec une ancienne Toile de Jouy au décor exotique.

→ The bathroom has not escaped the "decoration mania" of the lady of

the house, and, as expected, she has succeeded in combining comfort with decoration, as we see in the furniture and charming ornaments. • Michelles „Deko-Manie" ist auch das Badezimmer nicht entgangen, und wie zu erwarten auch hier eine gelungene Mischung aus Komfort, charmanten Objekten und überraschenden Möbeln. • La salle de bains n'a pas échappé à la « déco mania » de la maîtresse de maison et comme prévu elle a réussi à combiner le confort avec des meubles et des objets de charme.

HOUSE OF FRÉDÉRIC MISTRAL

HOUSE OF FRÉDÉRIC MISTRAL
MAILLANE

"Now my young man, I've done my duty. You know far more than anyone ever taught me!" These were the words Frédéric Mistral's father imparted to his son on learning he had just earned his law degree. At the age of 21, Mistral took an even more momentous decision, vowing to "revive a sense of race in Provence and bring about a resurrection by restoring the historic mother tongue of my country and bringing Provençal back into fashion with the flame of divine poetry." The author of the Provençal language dictionary, "Lou Trésor dóu Felibrige," and the epic poem, "Mirèio", was also renowned for founding Arles's famous museum of ethnography, the "Museon Arlaten". Mistral set up home in Maillane in 1876. "I'm currently surrounded by builders," he wrote to a friend, shortly afterwards, "I'm having a small but pleasantly comfortable house built in the garden you saw, looking out onto the Alpilles." In his last will and testament penned on 7 September 1907 the legendary poet left his property to the local commune, thus preserving his home for posterity. Mistral, whose motto was "Lou souléou me fai canta" – the sun makes me sing – may have passed away long ago, but his spirit still haunts this charming Provençal abode.

„Und nun, mein lieber Junge, habe ich meine Pflicht erfüllt. Du weißt viel mehr, als ich einst lernte", sprach Vater Mistral, als sein Sohn das Jurastudium abschloss. Mit 21 Jahren nahm sich Frédéric vor, „in der Provence das Gefühl für die eigene Herkunft neu zu wecken, durch die Wiederbelebung der Muttersprache und Geschichte meines Landes eine Wiedergeburt herbeiführen und das Provenzalische durch den Einfluss und die Flamme der göttlichen Poesie populär zu machen." Er schrieb das provenzalische Wörterbuch „Lou Trésor dóu Felibrige", das herrliche Versepos „Mirèio", gründete das „Museon Arlaten", das ethnografische Museum von Arles, und zog 1876 nach Maillane. „Ich bin derzeit von Maurern umgeben", schrieb er an einen Freund, „Ich lasse mir ein kleines, aber bequemes und hübsches Haus im Garten bauen, den Sie kennen, mit Blick auf die Alpilles." In seinem Testament vom 7. September 1907 vermachte der Dichter seinen Besitz der Gemeinde Maillane und sorgte so dafür, dass das Haus der Nachwelt erhalten blieb. „Lou souléou me fai canta" – die Sonne bringt mich zum Singen – war Mistrals Motto: In seinem schönen provenzalischen Haus scheint seine Stimme heute noch lebendig zu sein.

« Maintenant mon beau gars, moi j'ai fait mon devoir. Tu en sais beaucoup plus que ce qu'on m'a appris », dit le père de Frédéric Mistral à son fils qui venait d'obtenir sa licence de droit. À 21 ans, le jeune Mistral prend la résolution de « raviver en Provence le sentiment de race, provoquer une résurrection par la restauration de la langue maternelle et historique de mon pays, rendre la vogue au provençal par l'influx et la flamme de la divine poésie ». Auteur du « Trésor dóu Felibrige », un dictionnaire de la langue provençale, de l'inoubliable poème épique « Mirèio », et créateur du célèbre musée ethnographique arlésien, le « Museon Arlaten », Mistral s'établit à Maillane en 1876. « Je suis actuellement au milieu des maçons – écrit-il à un ami – « Je me fais bâtir une maison petite mais commode et agréable, dans le jardin que vous connaissez, en face des Alpilles ». Dans son testament du 7 septembre 1907 le grand poète lègue sa propriété à la commune de Maillane, préservant ainsi sa maison pour la postérité. Celui qui avait pour devise « Lou souléou me fai canta » nous a quitté, mais son ombre rôde toujours dans cette belle demeure provençale.

← and PP. 120–121 This house preserves the vestiges of a bygone era. Pushing back the ancient wooden door, visitors discover the comfortable circumstances of a well-to-do Provençal family. • Das ganze Haus zeugt von der Lebensart vergangener Zeiten und gewährt uns einen kurzen Blick in die plüschige Behaglichkeit einer wohlsituierten Familie. • Cette maison témoigne de l'art de vivre d'une certaine époque et nous fait entrer dans le monde quotidien et l'ambiance feutrée d'une famille aisée.

P. 123 In 1876 Mistral had a new house built at 12 Avenue Lamartine in Maillane in view of his upcoming marriage to Marie Louise Rivière. In his own words, it was "convenient and pleasant". • Im Jahre 1876 ließ Mistral ein neues Haus erbauen – „bequem und angenehm", mit seinen eigenen Worten –, in der Nummer 12 der Avenue Lamartine im Dorf Maillane. Anlass war die Hochzeit mit seiner Verlobten Marie Louise Rivière. • En 1876 Mistral fit construire une nouvelle maison – « commode et agréable », selon ses propres mots – au

12 Avenue Lamartine à Maillane et cela en vue de son mariage avec sa fiancée Marie Louise Rivière.

↑ The dining room is decorated with beautiful old Provençal furniture and local faïences. • Das Speisezimmer mit seinen schönen provenzalischen Möbeln und Fayencen aus der Region. • La salle à manger abrite de beaux meubles provençaux et des faïences régionales.

125

↑ Everything has been preserved in the "Museon", and you could almost believe that the great poet will push open the door of his beautiful house at any minute... • Alles im „Museon" ist so gut erhalten, dass der Besucher meinen mag, der große Dichter könnte jederzeit eine der Türen aufstoßen und den Raum betreten ... • Tout a été préservé dans le « Museon » et le visiteur a l'impression que le grand poète va pousser la porte de sa belle demeure d'une minute à l'autre.

→ Was this the writing desk where the master wrote "Mireio", his epic poem in the Provençal language, which tells the tragic love story of a girl from a good family and a poor basketmaker? • Hat der Meister-Dichter an diesem Schreib-tisch sein episches Gedicht „Mireio" verfasst, das in rein provenzalischem Dialekt von der tragischen Liebe einer Tochter aus gutem Haus und einem armen Korbflechter erzählt? • Est-ce à ce bureau que le maître écrivit le poème épique en langue provençale qu'il nomma « Mireio » et qui raconte l'histoire d'amour tragique entre une fille de bonne famille et un pauvre vannier ?

↑ The bedroom is a window on the past. Nothing gives away the 21st-century reality which lies behind its walls. • Das Schlafzimmer ist wie ein Fenster in die Vergangenheit, und es scheint, als bleibe unsere heutige Realität außerhalb seiner Mauern. • La chambre à coucher est une fenêtre sur le passé et rien ne trahit la réalité du 21ᵉ siècle au-delà des murs.

→ This washstand, just off the main bedroom, is a picture of monastic simplicity. • Die Waschecke gleich neben dem Schlafzimmer besticht durch klösterliche Einfachheit. • Situé à côté de la chambre à coucher, le coin toilette étonne par son caractère monacal.

L'HÔTEL DE BOURNISSAC

L'HÔTEL DE BOURNISSAC
CHRISTIAN TORTU
NOVES

The Hôtel de Bournissac is an austere-looking 17th-century mansion in Noves, a sleepy southern French town haunted by the ghosts of Laura and Petrarch. After centuries of pomp and splendour, the house fell into disuse and suffered years of neglect. The new owner, Christian Tortu, has respected its venerable age and undertaken a renovation which has not altered the original patina. Nor has he touched the walls' flaking paintwork or stirred centuries of noble dust. Tortu is an artist, an inspired florist and creative arranger with a gift for bringing out the beauty in bouquets of twigs, rose-petal-covered lampshades, or unusual organic arrangements which prove that fruit and vegetable matter are as much a part of his artistic vocabulary as flowers. Tortu has brought an artist's eye to his Noves home, preserving the Bournissac's beautiful Zuber wallpaper and its antique curtains and leaving the worn floorboards exactly as they are. These decorative touches bear witness to the passing fads and fashions the house has lived through in its history. This magical place, charged with genuine atmosphere, proves that one does not necessarily have to destroy the past to create new beauty.

Das Hôtel de Bournissac ist ein strenges Gebäude aus dem 17. Jahrhundert im ruhigen Noves, das immer noch den Geist von Laura und Petrarca verströmt. Das Haus durchlebte glanzvolle Zeiten, wurde später vernachlässigt und verfiel zu guter Letzt. Der neue Besitzer Christian Tortu ist dennoch entschlossen, das hohe Alter des Hauses zu ehren: abblätternde Farbe und erlesene Patina bleiben unangetastet. Tortu ist Künstler, einfallsreicher Florist mit dem genialen Talent, Schönheit hervorzulocken: Ein Bündel Zweige, ein mit getrockneten Rosenblüten übersäter Lampenschirm oder ein ausgefallenes Arrangement mit Obst und Gemüse gehören ebenso zu seinem Repertoire wie Blumengebinde. In Tortus Haus in Noves werden die Zuber-Tapeten mit ihren atemberaubenden Panoramen noch ebenso in Ehren gehalten wie die alten Vorhänge, die wurmstichigen Dielen und jener Zierrat, der von all den Vorlieben und Modeerscheinungen zeugt, die dieses Haus kommen und gehen sah. Tortu gelang es, einen magischen Ort, eine unvergessliche Atmosphäre herzustellen. Seine Art, Schönes zu schaffen, ohne Bestehendes zu zerstören, dürfte einzigartig sein.

L'Hôtel de Bournissac, une sévère bâtisse datant du 17ᵉ siècle à Noves – un village tranquille où rôdent les fantômes de Laure et de Pétrarque –, a connu des siècles de faste et des années d'abandon et de négligence. Son nouveau propriétaire Christian Tortu a décidé de respecter son âge vénérable et de ne pas toucher à ses patines, à ses peintures écaillées et à sa poussière ennoblie par le temps. Tortu est un artiste, un fleuriste iconoclaste et un créateur inspiré qui a le don de mettre au jour la beauté d'un bouquet de branches, d'un abat-jour couvert de pétales de roses séchées ou d'une composition hors du commun qui prouve que les fruits et les légumes font autant partie de son vocabulaire artistique que les fleurs. Dans sa maison de Noves, Tortu s'est bien gardé de toucher aux papiers peints Zuber, des panoramiques d'une beauté impressionnante. Il a préservé pieusement les rideaux anciens, les planchers vermoulus et tout un ensemble d'éléments décoratifs qui témoignent des goûts et des modes que sa maison a vu défiler. Le résultat ? Un endroit magique. Une ambiance inoubliable. Et une démarche exemplaire qui prouve qu'on peut créer la beauté sans détruire.

PP. 130–131 Secluded behind impressively high stone walls, Christian Tortu's garden is a haven of peace and tranquillity. • Im Garten findet Christian Tortu Frieden und Stille hinter den beeindruckend hohen Mauern. • Le jardin clos de murs d'une hauteur impressionnante offre à Christian Tortu la paix et le silence.

P. 133 In the entrance hall, a classical vase made of woven branches, designed by Tortu, sits on an antique sculptor's stand. • Auf einem alten Bildhauer-schemel im Eingangsbereich steht eine von Tortu gefertigte klassische Vase aus Zweigen. • Dans l'entrée, un vase classique à base de branches signé Tortu a trouvé sa place sur une sellette de sculpteur ancienne.

↑ No trace of furniture in the reception room looking out over the garden. The aesthetic eye needs no distraction from the beauty of the colourwash. • Im sparsam möblierten großen Salon zur Gartenseite hin begnügt sich der Ästhet mit der Schönheit der Wandfarbe. • Peu de meubles dans la grande salle d'apparat donnant sur le jardin. L'esthète se contente de la beauté du badigeon.

→ The dining room door opens onto a vista of antique panoramic wallpaper designed by Zuber. • Die Türen zum Speisesaal öffnen sich zwischen originalen Panoramatapeten der renommierten Manufaktur Zuber. • La porte de la salle à manger s'ouvre sur des parois décorées avec des papiers peints panoramiques d'époque signés Zuber.

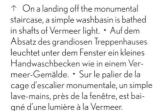

↑ On a landing off the monumental staircase, a simple washbasin is bathed in shafts of Vermeer light. • Auf dem Absatz des grandiosen Treppenhauses leuchtet unter dem Fenster ein kleines Handwaschbecken wie in einem Vermeer-Gemälde. • Sur le palier de la cage d'escalier monumentale, un simple lave-mains, près de la fenêtre, est baigné d'une lumière à la Vermeer.

→ Tortu came up with the innovative idea of leaving much of the house in its original state. Stone and wood patinas, floors and curtains, were left unchanged. • Tortu beließ einen großen Teil des Hauses im Originalzustand: Patina, Vertäfelungen, Böden und Vorhänge. • Tortu a eu l'idée originale de laisser une grande partie de la maison en l'état : patines, boiseries, sols et rideaux.

LA MAISON DOMAINE DE BOURNISSAC

LA MAISON DOMAINE DE BOURNISSAC

PALUDS DE NOVES

This old country inn located in the heart of Provence is just minutes from the town of Saint-Rémy. It is still quite a secret place, even in this much-explored area. At the end of a long gravel road, hidden away, this simple house comes into view. Yet the Domaine de Bournissac has a deceptive exterior; the inside is not quite as simple as it appears to be. The centuries-old farmhouse has been restored and revived as an oasis of calm. The expert pairing of style and simplicity is unmistakable in these surroundings. Pale colours of marble, stone and bleached wood signal the restful atmosphere to be found within its walls. Every room is different; each one in a muted palette and composed by a sure and artistic hand. Outside, the delightful garden and terrace grant space to sit in the sun and dream, or offer welcome shade cast by a massive old oak tree. In the summer, fields of sunflowers and lavender are in bloom. This is the landscape and light that so inspired Vincent van Gogh, and lures people to Provence still.

Nur wenige Minuten von Saint-Rémy im Herzen der Provence liegt ein alter Landgasthof. Er ist sogar in dieser touristisch weitgehend erschlossenen Gegend ein Geheimtipp geblieben. Versteckt am Ende eines langen Kieswegs entdeckt man plötzlich ein einfaches Haus. Doch dieser Eindruck täuscht: Die Domaine de Bournissac wirkt nur äußerlich einfach. Das ehemalige, mehrere Jahrhunderte alte Bauernhaus ist heute als Oase der Stille wieder zum Leben erwacht. Stil und Schlichtheit sind eine perfekte Symbiose eingegangen. Die blasse Farbpalette von Marmor, Stein und gebleichtem Holz signalisiert, welch entspannende Atmosphäre innerhalb der Steinmauern zu finden ist. Die Gästezimmer wurden jeweils individuell gestaltet, alle jedoch gekonnt und stilsicher und in warmen Farben gehalten. Draußen laden Garten und Terrasse zum Sonnenbaden und Träumen ein, und eine riesige alte Eiche spendet angenehmen Schatten. Im Sommer blühen Sonnenblumen und Lavendel in den Feldern ringsherum. Landschaft und Licht inspirierten einst Vincent van Gogh und ziehen bis heute die Menschen an.

À quelques minutes à peine de Saint-Rémy, en plein coeur de la Provence, se dresse une vieille auberge de campagne. C'est un endroit encore secret dans cette région qui n'en compte plus guère. Tout au bout d'une longue route de gravier surgit une maison toute simple. Mais que l'on ne s'y trompe pas : l'intérieur est beaucoup moins modeste qu'il n'y paraît. Cette ancienne ferme séculaire a été restaurée, transformée en une oasis de tranquillité, où raffinement et simplicité vont de pair. Les teintes discrètes du marbre, de la pierre et du bois brut annoncent l'atmosphère paisible qui règne entre ses murs. Chaque chambre est différente des autres, mais toutes sont dotées de couleurs douces et décorées avec beaucoup de goût. À l'extérieur, le jardin et la terrasse se prêtent au repos et à la rêverie, à l'ombre d'un imposant chêne centenaire. En été, les champs de tournesol et de lavande déploient leurs symphonies de couleurs. C'est le paysage et la lumière qui ont inspiré Vincent van Gogh, et qui continuent d'attirer les visiteurs.

PP. 138–139 At sunset, the ochre-coloured soil of Provence exudes the heat accumulated during the day and the countryside is covered in a light, yellowish mist. • Bei Sonnenuntergang entsteigt der Landschaft ein leichter gelblicher Nebel, und die ockerfarbene Erde der Provence gibt die aufgestaute Hitze des Tages frei. • Au coucher de soleil, la terre ocrée de la Provence dégage la chaleur accumulée pendant la journée et le paysage se couvre d'une légère brume jaunâtre.

P. 141 Who hasn't dreamed of sitting on the terrace of an old farmhouse, in the shade of an ancient, majestic fig tree and enjoying a peaceful, restful moment? • Haben Sie auch schon einmal

davon geträumt, sich auf der Terrasse eines alten Bauernhofes zu erholen, im Schatten eines majestätischen Feigenbaums, der wahrscheinlich hunderte Jahre alt ist? • Qui n'a pas rêvé de s'asseoir sur la terrasse d'un vieux mas, dans l'ombre d'un majestueux figuier séculaire et de profiter d'un moment paisible et reposant ?

↑ In the gourmet restaurant, a chandelier of Baroque ironwork lights up the tables and chairs of wrought iron. A kitchen dresser of light-coloured wood harmonises with the whiteness of the walls. • Im ausgezeichneten Restaurant wirft ein Kronleuchter aus barockem Eisenwerk sein Licht auf Tische und Stühle, die ebenfalls aus Eisen gearbeitet sind.

Ein Geschirrschrank aus hellem Holz harmoniert aufs Angenehmste mit der weißen Farbe der Wände. • Dans le restaurant gastronomique, un lustre en ferronnerie baroque éclaire des tables et des chaises en fer forgé. Un vaisselier en bois clair s'harmonise avec la couleur blanche des murs.

→ Ceramic cutwork bells – decorative and useful at the same time – form a pretty still life. • Die Glocken aus durchbrochener Keramik sind zugleich dekorativ und nützlich. Sie ergeben ein hübsches Stillleben. • Des cloches en céramique ajourée, à la fois décoratives et utiles, forment une jolie nature morte .

↑ White walls, white linen, white ceramics: the "Blanche" room honours the colour white. • Weiße Wände, weiße Wäsche und weiße Keramik: das „Weiße Zimmer" ist dieser reinen Farbe gewidmet. • Murs blancs, linge blanc, céramique blanche : dans la chambre nommée « Blanche » le blanc est à l'honneur.

→ The bed, curtains and furnishings are executed in an intentionally monochrome palette. The mood of lightness is worthy of the beautiful room name "Organdie". • Die bewusst monochrom gehaltene Palette dieses Zimmers umfasst das Bett, die Vorhänge und die Möbel. Es vermittelt einen Eindruck von Leichtigkeit, dem sich der schöne Name "Organdy" verdankt. • La palette volontairement monochrome de cette chambre s'empare du lit, des rideaux et du mobilier. Sa légèreté lui a valu le beau nom d' «Organdi ».

PP. 146–147 The twin beds and the matching seats are painted a pearly grey and are modelled on a rustic piece of 18th-century furniture. The bouquets of dried herbs hanging in a row on the wall perfume the air with the delicious scents of Provence. • Die beiden Betten und die dazugehörigen Bänke sind von bäuerlichem Mobiliar des 18. Jahrhunderts inspiriert und in Perlgrau gehalten. Das Zimmer ist mit dem köstlichen Duft der Provence parfümiert, der den Bündeln getrockneter Kräuter an der Wand entströmt. • Les lits-jumeaux et leurs banquettes assorties sont peintes en gris perle et leur modèle s'inspire d'un mobi-

lier campagnard d'époque 18e. Les bouquets d'herbes séchées qui s'alignent sur le mur parfument l'air avec les délicieuses senteurs de Provence.

← A hamper of braided twine, a retro piece of washstand furniture painted white, and walls covered in a blue wash perfectly convey the natural aspect of the decorative style. • Die Natürlichkeit der Einrichtung spiegelt sich perfekt in einem aus Kordel geflochtenen Korb, dem weiß gestrichenen alten Waschtisch und der blauen „al-fresco"-Wandbemalung. • Un panier en corde tressée, un meuble lavabo « rétro » peint

en blanc et des murs couverts d'un lavis bleu traduisent parfaitement le côté « naturel » de la décoration.

↑ At the Domaine de Bournissac the blue and white decor of a room obviously named "La Bleue" provides a gentle atmosphere that lulls you to sleep. • Im blau-weißen Dekor des so passend „La Bleue" benannten Zimmers der Domaine de Bournissac kann man sich getrost zur Ruhe betten. • Au Domaine de Bournissac, on s'endort dans le décor bleu et blanc d'une chambre baptisée de toute évidence « La Bleue ».

JEAN-CLAUDE BRIALY

JEAN-CLAUDE BRIALY
SAINT-RÉMY-DE-PROVENCE

It's already more than 20 years since the late Jean-Claude Brialy bought a house at Eygalières. The actor often repeated that at the time it was "the spitten image of a modest gatekeeper's house". The renowned French actor and film director, one of the leading figures of the Nouvelle Vague, made his screen presence felt in Claude Chabrol's "The Cousins". It was around this same period that Brialy first discovered Provence. The actor hesitated a little too long over his original project of buying an 'hôtel particulier' in Saint-Rémy-de-Provence, but he finally settled in the region in 1995, after sending his friend Bruno off to find "a home to retire to". Working in collaboration with the architect Hugues Bosc and landscape gardener Michel Semini, Brialy's 1900-style house – an anonymous-looking villa surrounded by wasteland – was transformed into a stunning home filled with mementoes the actor has accumulated in the course of his career and his trips around the world. "I knew exactly what I wanted," said Brialy. "A big sun-filled kitchen painted Van Gogh yellow. A spacious Provençal living-room, a pool which wouldn't look 'nouveau riche' but blended into the garden like a natural pond. And I wanted a garden that would stay green all year round." Jean-Claude and Bruno's home is all this and more!

Wenn man Jean-Claude Brialy Glauben schenkt, war dieses Haus, das er vor mehr als 20 Jahren erwarb, zuvor das heruntergekommene Heim eines Bahnwärters. Als einer der Stars der Nouvelle Vague ist der inzwischen verstorbene Schauspieler und Regisseur auch heute noch im Begriff, nicht zuletzt wegen seiner atemberaubenden Präsenz in Filmen wie „Schrei, wenn du kannst" von Claude Chabrol. In jener Zeit verliebte er sich in die Provence. Bei einem Stadthaus in Saint-Rémy-de-Provence zögerte er etwas zu lange, doch die zweite Chance kam 1995, als er seinen Freund Bruno auf die Suche nach einem „Altersruhesitz" schickte. Mit Hilfe des Architekten Hugues Bosc und des Landschaftsgärtners Michel Semini verwandelte sich das Jahrhundertwende-Haus – ein anonymer Klotz mit Grundstück – in ein charmantes Domizil voller Erinnerungen. „Ich wusste genau, was ich wollte", erzählte Brialy: „Eine große, helle Küche in van-Gogh-Gelb. Einen großen provenzalischen Salon. Einen Pool, der nicht neureich wirken sollte, sondern wie ein Gartenteich. Und natürlich einen immergrünen Garten." Für Jean-Claude und Bruno wurde der Traum Wirklichkeit.

Si l'on en croit Jean-Claude Brialy, sa belle maison provençale était il y a une vingtaine d'années qu'une vilaine maison de garde-barrière. On revoit le célèbre acteur et réalisateur, figure de proue de la Nouvelle Vague, crevant l'écran dans « Les cousins » de Claude Chabrol. C'est à cette époque qu'il découvrit la Provence. Il hésita trop longtemps à acheter un hôtel particulier à Saint-Rémy-de-Provence, mais il a eu sa revanche en 1995 après avoir demandé à son ami Bruno de partir à la recherche d'une « maison de retraité ». Avec l'aide de l'architecte Hugues Bosc et du paysagiste Michel Semini, la maison de style 1900 – un pavillon anonyme entouré d'un terrain vague – est devenue une demeure charmante qui abrite des souvenirs accumulés tout au long d'une brillante carrière et au fil de voyages à travers le monde. « Je savais ce que je voulais » racontait Brialy. « Une grande cuisine claire, jaune comme le jaune Van Gogh. Un grand salon provençal et une piscine qui ne ferait pas 'nouveau riche' mais ressemblerait à un bassin de jardin. Et puis un jardin vert toute l'année ». Jean-Claude et Bruno ont réalisé leur rêve.

PP. 150–151 Working in collaboration with the architect and landscape gardener Michel Semini, Jean-Claude and Bruno have transformed a former wasteland into a luxuriant garden. An equally incredible metamorphosis had been effected on the house, which began life as a suburban bungalow but is now a magnificent Provençal villa. • Mithilfe des Landschaftsarchitekten Michel Semini machten Jean-Claude und Bruno aus einer Brachfläche einen bezaubernden Garten. Die gleiche Metamorphose durchlief auch das Gebäude, das seine Karriere als banales Wohnhaus begann und sich heute als bildschöne provenzalische Villa präsentiert. • Avec l'aide de l'architecte-paysagiste Michel Semini, Jean-Claude

et Bruno avaient transforméun terrain vague en un jardin plein de charme. La métamorphose fait écho à celle de la maison qui commença sa carrière comme pavillon de banlieue et resplendit aujourd'hui de toute sa beauté de villa provençale.

P. 153 The shutters of the actor's bedroom open out onto stunning views of the garden. • Von seinem Schlafzimmer aus schaute Brialy in den herrlichen Garten. • De sa chambre, le comédien avait une vue imprenable sur le jardin.

← White-lacquered cane furniture and wrought-iron tables turn the terrace and its overhanging arbour into an elegant open-air dining room. • Weiße Rattan-

möbel und schmiedeeiserne Tischchen machen die schattig belaubte Terrasse zu einem Freiluftsalon. • Des meubles en rotin laqué blanc et des tables en fer forgé transforment la terrasse et sa tonnelle en un salon de plein air.

↑ Jean-Claude Brialy disliked the electric blue of Californian swimming pools and has transformed his own into a natural stretch of water. • Jean-Claude Brialy verabscheute die stahlblauen kalifornischen Pools. Sein eigenes Schwimmbecken wirkt wie ein natürlicher Teich. • Jean-Claude Brialy abhorrait les piscines californiennes bleu électrique. Il avait transformé la sienne en plan d'eau.

↑ In Jean-Claude's bed-room, 18th-century wood panelling in striking shades of absinthe reflect the intense southern light. Beyond the landing, a glimpse of Bruno's room furnished with a rustic four-poster bed. • Die Wände in Jean-Claudes Schlafzimmer sind mit leuchtend absinthgrünen Vertäfelungen aus dem 18. Jahrhundert bedeckt. Auf der anderen Flurseite erspäht man in Brunos Schlafzimmer das rustikale, weiß bezogene Himmelbett. • Dans la chambre de Jean-Claude, des boiseries 18e couleur d'absinthe habillent les parois et captent la lumière. Au-delà du palier, on aperçoit la chambre de Bruno et son lit à baldaquin rustique habillé de blanc.

→ The intense light of the Midi filters through an elegant embroidered curtain in the bedroom. • Im Schlafzimmer dämpft eine bestickte Gardine das grelle Licht Südfrankreichs. • Dans la chambre à coucher, un rideau orné de broderies filtre la lumière intense du Midi.

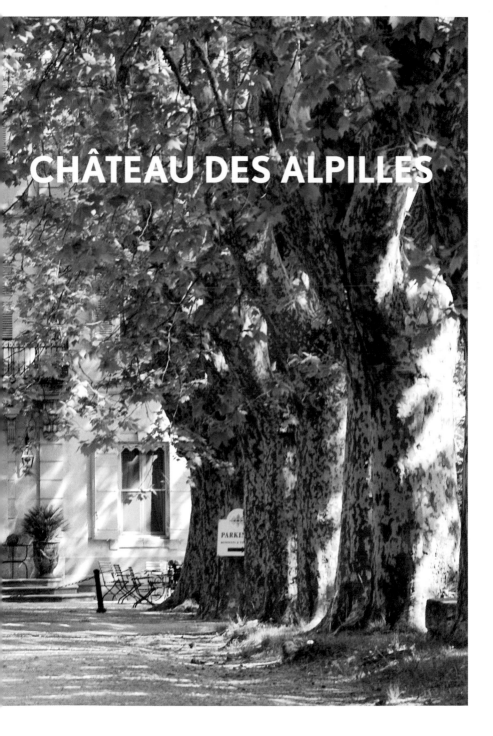

CHÂTEAU DES ALPILLES

CHÂTEAU DES ALPILLES
SAINT-RÉMY-DE-PROVENCE

This country residence was once owned by the family of French writer Amédée Pichot, whose guests included politicians and artists. Now a hotel run by a mother-and-daughter team, the château nonetheless remains a destination for "le tout Paris." For most, a walk in the enchanting park is the first priority on arrival. Covering 17 acres, this estate on the edge of the Alpine foothills is full of old plane trees and secret places that will leave you yearning for a bit of Proust – a feeling that only intensifies when sitting in front of the fire (there's one in every room), surrounded by antiques. Thankfully, there are more contemporary diversions on offer too – the modern Provençal cuisine, for instance, or the pool by which guests can enjoy something probably unknown to Proust and his peers: chilling out.

Einst gehörte dieser Landsitz der Familie des Schriftstellers Amédée Pichot, der hier französische Politiker und Künstler zu Gast hatte. Heute empfängt ein Mutter-Tochter-Gespann die Gäste, zu denen immer noch „tout Paris" gehört. Noch vor dem Kofferauspacken steht für die meisten ein Spaziergang durch den zauberhaften Park an. Am Fuß der Voralpen erstreckt sich auf sieben Hektar diese bemerkenswerte Anlage; alte Platanen und viele klandestine Plätzchen zum Verweilen sorgen für das dringende Verlangen, anschließend Proust zu lesen. Ein Gefühl, das im Herrenhaus, mit seinen Antiquitäten und einem Kamin in jedem Zimmer, nicht gerade schwächer wird. Nur gut, dass es dann doch ein bisschen zeitgenössische Ablenkung gibt – die moderne provenzalische Küche des Hauses etwa, oder einen Pool, wo man etwas tut, das es zu Prousts Zeiten noch gar nicht gab: relaxen.

Cette propriété appartenait autrefois à la famille de l'écrivain Amédée Pichot, qui accueillait ici des personnalités du monde politique et artistique. Aujourd'hui, un duo mère-fille y reçoit encore le Tout-Paris. Avant même de défaire ses bagages, on se doit de faire une promenade dans le magnifique parc de sept hectares qui s'étend au pied des Alpilles. Ses platanes et ses nombreux refuges ombragés invitent à la rêverie et suscitent le besoin urgent de relire Proust; et ce besoin n'en est que plus vif quand on pénètre à l'intérieur de l'hôtel meublé d'antiquités, dont chaque chambre dispose d'une cheminée. Par bonheur, les plaisirs contemporains ne sont pas tout à fait exclus, l'établissement proposant notamment de la cuisine provençale moderne et une piscine où s'adonner à une activité encore inconnue au temps de Proust : la relaxation.

PP. 158–159 A magnificent drive leads to the Château des Alpilles. The imposing silhouettes of the hundred-year-old plane trees frame the façade, a viewthat seems to spring from an Old Master. • Eine prachtvolle Allee führt zum Chateau des Alpilles. Die imposanten Silhouetten der hundert Jahre alten Platanen rahmen den Blick auf die Fassade des Schlosses, fast wie in einem alten Gemälde. • Une magnifique allée mène vers le Château des Alpilles et les silhouettes imposantes des platanes centenaires encadrent la vue sur la façade à la façon d'un tableau ancien.

P. 161 Opposite the pretty, tree-filled park they have set up tables to allow the guests to dine in an elegant setting, far away from the noises of the town. • Im Angesicht der hübschen Bäume des Parks sind die Tische schon für die Gäste gedeckt, weit entfernt vom Lärm der Stadt, in einer eleganten Umgebung. • Face au joli parc arboré, on a dressé les tables pour permettre aux hôtes de prendre leurs repas dans un cadre raffiné, loin des bruits de la ville.

PP. 162–163 The pool has a screen of greenery composed of trees and pot plants. You're in Provence, and so it's not unusual for the swimmers to gather round the pool for an al fresco meal. • Das Schwimmbecken ist von einer Wand aus Bäumen und großen Topfpflanzen umgeben. Hier in der Provence ist es nicht unüblich, dass sich die Badegäste ums Becken herum zu einem Verwöhn-Lunch sammeln. • La piscine s'entoure d'un écran de verdure composé d'arbres et de plantes en pot. On est en Provence et il n'est pas rare que les nageurs vont s'installer autour du bassin pour se régaler d'un repas au grand air.

P. 164 A French window with louvered shutters and a balcony which overlooks the foliage of an old plane tree... who can resist the charm of this perfectly romantic setting? • Eine Terrassentür mit eleganten Blenden, und dann der Balkon, mit Blick aufs Blattwerk der alten Platane – kann man so viel romantischem Charme widerstehen? • Une porte-fenêtre avec des volets à jalousies et un balcon qui donne sur le feuillage d'un vieux platane... qui peut résister au charme de ce cadre romantique à souhait ?

P. 165 The classical architecture of this lovely country seat has nothing ostentatious about it, and the surrounding park echoes its timeless beauty. • Die klassische Architektur des Herrenhauses wirkt zurückhaltend, und der Park, der es umgibt, spiegelt dessen zeitlose Schönheit. • L'architecture classique de cette belle gentilhommière n'a rien d'ostentatoire et le parc qui l'entoure fait écho à sa beauté intemporelle.

PP. 166–167 In the 19th century, such famous guests as Chateaubriand and Lamartine stayed in the château. In the dining room, the owners have chosen to keep the decor of the period. The Knoll tables and chairs are, in contrast, a bold, contemporary ensemble. • Im 19. Jahrhundert waren Berühmtheiten wie Chateaubriand und Lamartine zu Gast im Schloss, und im Speisesaal des Restaurants ist das Dekor dieser Epoche bewahrt worden. Aber die Tische und Stühle aus dem Hause Knoll sind entschieden zeitgenössisch. • Au 19e siècle des hôtes célèbres comme Chateaubriand et Lamartine séjournèrent dans le château, et dans la salle à manger du restaurant on a choisi de préserver le décor d'époque. Les tables et les chaises Knoll forment eux un ensemble résolument contemporain.

← In one of the rooms the owners have kept the bare brick walls and simply painted them white. A king-size bed takes up almost the whole of the space. • In diesem Zimmer sind die blanken Mauersteine direkt mit Weiß übermalt worden, und ein King-Size-Bett dominiert den Raum. • Dans une des chambres, les murs en briques nues ont été peints en blanc. Un lit « King Size » occupe presque toute la place.

↑ When the evenings become cool in Provence, there is no greater luxury than an open fire. At Château des Alpilles all the rooms are equipped with working fireplaces to make staying in the hotel as comfortable as possible. • Wenn die Abende in der Provence kühler werden, gibt es keinen größeren Luxus als ein prasselndes Kaminfeuer. Alle Zimmer im Château des Alpilles sind mit Kaminen ausgestattet, für den Komfort der

Gäste. • Quand les soirées en Provence se font fraîches il n'y a pas de plus grand luxe qu'un feu de cheminée. Au Château des Alpilles, toutes les chambres sont équipées de cheminées pour que le séjour des hôtes soit confortable.

LE MAS D'ESTO

LE MAS D'ESTO
SIKI OF SOMALIA
SAINT-RÉMY-DE-PROVENCE

Princess Siki of Somalia is a fascinating lady and every inch a princess. Siki creates jewellery which combines the brilliance of gold with stones of unusual cut and shape and a touch of exoticism inspired by her African origins. Since she loves the countryside, she escapes Paris whenever she can to take refuge at her estate near Saint-Rémy-de-Provence. Affectionately dubbed La Principessa by her closest friends, Siki tells how these same friends also chose the name of "Trianon Rose" for her ivy-covered, pink-ochre country house. The princess sees no reason why her sophisticated Parisian lifestyle should impinge on this old "mas", a typical Provençal farmhouse. Here, the ambience is as simple as can be and it is like stepping into one of Colette's novels. This is the perfect place to emulate that author and curl up in a wicker chair to sip "vin d'orange". For the interior, Siki has chosen stucco walls tinted with pink ochre, and solid country-style furniture. The only notes of sophistication: Siki's bedroom with its 1940s' bed surmounted with a canopy, and the discreet presence of her King Charles spaniels, Greta and Frégoli.

Siki de Somalie trägt nicht nur den Titel, sondern ist der Inbegriff einer Prinzessin. Siki entwirft Schmuck, wobei Gold mit ungewöhnlich geschliffenen oder geformten Steinen und einem exotischen Touch, der auf ihre afrikanischen Wurzeln zurückgeht, kombiniert wird. Als große Naturliebhaberin flieht sie sooft wie möglich aus Paris in ihr Landhaus bei Saint-Rémy-de-Provence. Die „Principessa", wie sie von guten Freunden genannt wird, erzählt lächelnd, dass ihr efeu-bewachsenes, ockerrosa Landhaus denselben Freunden seinen Namen „Trianon Rose" verdankt. Ihr mondänes Pariser Leben müsse nicht auf ihr altes „mas", das provenzalische Bauernhaus, abfärben, findet die Prinzessin. Im einfach gehaltenen Ambiente fühlt man sich in einen Colette-Roman versetzt und bekommt Lust, es sich hier mit einem Glas „vin d'orange" im Korbsessel bequem zu machen. Das Innere des Hauses wird von den in Ockerrosa gestrichenen Wänden und soliden Möbeln bestimmt. Mondänes Flair verbreiten nur das Bett mit dem Baldachin aus den 1940er-Jahren in Sikis Zimmer und die diskrete Gegenwart der King-Charles-Spaniel Greta und Frégoli.

Siki de Somalie n'est pas seulement princesse de par son titre, elle l'est aussi par sa personnalité fascinante. Siki crée des bijoux qui marient l'éclat de l'or avec des pierres aux tailles et aux formes inhabituelles et avec une touche d'exotisme inspiré par ses origines africaines. Comme elle aime la nature, elle fuit Paris aussi souvent que possible pour se réfugier dans son domaine du côté de Saint-Rémy-de-Provence. La Principessa, c'est ainsi que l'ont baptisée ses amis intimes, raconte, avec le sourire, que ces mêmes amis ont aussi donné le surnom de « Trianon Rose » à sa maison de campagne couleur ocre rose, enfouie sous le lierre. La princesse ne voit d'ailleurs pas très bien pourquoi la sophistication de son existence parisienne viendrait teinter ses séjours dans ce mas ancien avec sa grande terrasse couverte et son champ de verveine. Chez elle, l'ambiance est plutôt à la simplicité ; on se croirait dans un ouvrage de Colette et – comme l'écrivain – bien disposé à siroter du vin d'orange dans un siège en osier. Pour son intérieur, Siki a choisi des murs en stuc teintés d'ocre rosé et un mobilier solide et campagnard. Les seules notes sophistiquées : la chambre de Siki où trône un lit 1940 surmonté d'un baldaquin et la présence discrète de ses king-charles, Greta et Frégoli.

PP. 170–171 On the walls Siki has hung old straw hats and trays and, above the table, she has suspended a turn-of-the-century lamp. • An der Wand alte Strohhüte und Brotkörbe, über dem Tisch eine Lampe aus der Zeit der Jahrhundertwende. • Sur les murs Siki a accroché de vieux chapeaux et des plateaux en paille, et au-dessus de la table rustique elle a suspendu un luminaire fin de siècle.

P. 173 The table and benches await guests on the shady terrace. A wicker poultry basket has been transformed into a lamp. • Unter dem Terrassen-vordach warten die Bänke und der Tisch geduldig auf Gäste. Ein Vogelkäfig dient heute als Laterne. • Sous l'auvent de la terrasse, une table et des bancs attendent les invités. Une cage à volaille en osier s'est transformée en lanterne.

↑ The Mas d'Esto with its pink-ochre walls, red shutters and ivy-covered façade, a pastoral idyll in the heart of Provence. • Das Mas d'Esto mit den Wänden in Ockerrosa, roten Fenster-läden und der efeubewachsenen Fas-sade – eine ländliche Idylle im Herzen der Provence. • Le mas d'Esto avec ses murs ocre rosé, ses volets rouges et sa façade couverte de lierre – l'idylle pastorale au cœur de la Provence.

→ Garden furniture and pot plants sheltered from the burning sun. Siki and her family love to eat breakfast in the shadow of the house. • Gartenmöbel und Topfpflanzen sind vor der brennen-den Sonne geschützt. Siki und ihre Familie frühstücken gern hier im Schat-ten des Hauses. • Des meubles de jardin et des plantes en pots à l'écart du soleil brûlant. Siki et sa famille adorent prendre leur petit déjeuner à l'ombre de la maison.

← In a cosy corner, the old patina of a Provençal cabinet-bookcase accentuates the rose-ochre colour of the walls. • In einer Ecke des Wohnzimmers akzentuiert die Patina eines altmodischen Bücherschranks den rosa getönten Ocker der Wandbemalung. • Dans un coin du séjour la patine ancienne d'une armoire-bibliothèque provençale accentue la couleur ocre rose des murs.

↑ Rustic kitchen furniture, with oil lamps and a large faience tureen on the table. • Die Küche ist mit rustikalen Möbeln und Öllampen ausgestattet, auf dem Tisch steht eine große Deckelterrine aus Fayence. • Le mobilier rustique de la cuisine, les lampes à huile et la grande terrine en faïence sur la table.

→ Pink ochre stuccoed walls and sofas covered with brilliant red fabric add warmth to the "grand salon". • Wände in Ockerrosa und die in Rottönen gehaltenen Sofas und Bezugsstoffe schaffen eine behagliche Atmosphäre. • Des murs en stuc ocre rosé et des canapés recouverts d'un tissu à dominante rouge apportent une note de chaleur au grand salon.

← ↑ The King Charles spaniels have found themselves a sunny spot, leaving their mistress sole possession of the bedroom and the canopied 1940s' bed. • Die King-Charles-Spaniel haben eine Liege vereinnahmt und überlassen ihrer Herrin das Schlafzimmer mit dem baldachinbekrönten Bett aus den 1940er-Jahren. • Les king-charles de la princesse ont pris possession d'une méridienne, laissant à leur maîtresse la propriété exclusive de sa chambre à coucher au lit 1940 surmonté d'un baldaquin.

LA BASTIDE

LA BASTIDE
AU PIED DES ALPILLES,
SAINT-RÉMY-DE-PROVENCE

"Decorators generally regale listeners with the classic restoration tale which starts out with a dilapidated old ruin that ends up miraculously transformed into a stunning new home. But in this case, things worked the other way round!" says interior decorator Lisa Kessel, showing us round a superb 17th and 18th-century residence, situated in a picturesque village at the foot of the Alpilles. She has an extensive international clientele who swear by her experience and her expert eye for design. However, on this occasion she was somewhat taken aback when a client asked her to work contrary to her usual routine, transforming a house "in perfectly good condition" into a ruin (albeit a temporary one!) Plywood partitions, sliding glass doors and other "modern horrors" all had to go. The aim was to restore the magnificent Provençal 'bastide' to its original pale stone glory and 'hôtel particulier' luxury. In the process, Lisa managed to integrate antique furniture, period paintings and a superb collection of objets d'art which had been wasting away in storage. Decorator and client can rightfully claim Caesar's boast, "veni, vidi, vici," as their own!

„Innenarchitekten erzählen sonst immer die gleichen Geschichten von abenteuerlichen Restaurierungen, die mit einem uralten, verfallenen Gemäuer beginnen und der wundersamen Verwandlung in ein Traumhaus enden. Bei diesem Haus war es genau andersherum", erzählt die Innenarchitektin Lisa Kessel bei der Führung durch das herrliche Gebäude aus dem 17. und 18. Jahrhundert. Ihre internationale Kundschaft schätzt ihre Erfahrung und ihr stilsicheres Auge. Als eine Kundin von ihr verlangte, ein „wohlerhaltenes" Haus - vorübergehend - praktisch abzureißen, war sie zunächst leicht konsterniert. Doch es wäre unvorstellbar gewesen, all die „modernen" Scheußlichkeiten wie Wandpaneele oder gläserne Schiebetüren beizubehalten: Diese wunderbare „bastide" verdiente es, ihr ursprüngliches Flair zurückzuerlangen und wieder der noble Wohnsitz zu werden, der sie einst war. Eine Herausforderung war es auch, all die schönen alten Möbel, Gemälde und edlen Accessoires einzubeziehen, die in einem Lagerhaus auf ihr Comeback warteten. Cäsars Motto „veni, vidi, vici" dürfen Lisa und ihre Kundin nach dieser Arbeit wohl zu Recht reklamieren.

« D'habitude les décorateurs vous racontent l'histoire classique d'une restauration rocambolesque qui commence avec une vieille maison en ruine et se termine par la transformation miraculeuse en une demeure splendide. Mais dans le cas de cette maison c'était bien le contraire », raconte la décoratrice Lisa Kessel en faisant le tour guidé d'une splendide bâtisse datant du 17ᵉ et du 18ᵉ siècle située au cœur d'un charmant village au pied des Alpilles. Sa clientèle internationale jure par son expérience et son œil averti. Mais quand sa cliente lui a demandé de transformer - temporairement - en ruine une maison « en bon état », elle a un peu tiqué. En fait, il était impensable de garder des murs en contreplaqué, des portes coulissantes en verre et autres horreurs « modernes ». Il fallait restituer à cette magnifique bastide sa blondeur d'antan et son côté « hôtel particulier » luxueux. Intégrer les beaux meubles anciens, les tableaux et une collection d'objets de qualité qui dormaient dans un garde-meuble était un autre défi. Lisa et sa cliente peuvent reprendre à leur compte le « veni, vidi, vici » de César et se reposer sur des lauriers bien mérités.

PP. 182–183 and 185 The swimming pool at La Bastide is surrounded by an abundance of dense vegetation, and the covered terrace that overlooks it is weighed down by an avalanche of roses in white, the favourite colour of the lady of the house. • Das Schwimmbad von La Bastide ist umgeben von einer dichten, blühenden Vegetation, und die bedeckte Terrasse oberhalb des Schwimmbeckens wird von weißen

Rosen eingehegt. Weiß ist die Lieblingsfarbe der Herrin des Hauses. • La piscine de La Bastide est entourée d'une végétation dense et abondante et la terrasse couverte qui la domine croule sous le poids d'une avalanche de roses blanches, la couleur favorite de la maîtresse de maison.

← Michel Semini created a precise landscape design for the luxuriant gar-

den, but the lady of the house softened its strict lines with rose bushes. • Für den herrlichen Garten zeichnete Michel Semini einen strengen Entwurf, den die Dame des Hauses jedoch mit Rosenbüschen auflockerte. • Michel Semini a dessiné un plan rigoureux pour le magnifique jardin, mais la maîtresse de maison l'a adouci en plantant des rosiers.

P. 187 In the heavenly garden there is an embarrassment of choice for our chatelaine among the very beautiful old roses. She has a talent for creating delightful little bouquets. • Im paradiesischen Garten hat man die Qual der Wahl beim Anblick der wunderschonen historischen Rosensorten. Die Hausherrin selbst hat einen untrüglichen Instinkt bei der Zusammenstellung der lieblichsten Bouquets. • Dans le jardin paradisiaque on n'a que l'embarras du choix pour cueillir les plus belles roses anciennes et la maîtresse de maison possède le talent inné pour composer des petits bouquets ravissants.

↑ Behind a collection of old watering cans, you'll discover a sign with the English translation of Claude Monet's famous maxim: "More than anything I must have flowers, always, always..." • Hinter einer kleinen Ansammlung von Gießkannen findet sich eine Tafel mit einer Maxime des berühmten Claude Monet: „Ich brauche Blumen, mehr als alles andere, jederzeit, immer ..." • Derrière une collection de vieux arrosoirs on découvre un écriteau avec la traduction anglaise de la célèbre maxime de Claude Monet : « More than anything I must have flowers, always, always... »

→ A high wall and an iron gate protect the garden from the inquisitive eyes of the curious. On a garden table, fruit and flowers form a charming still life. • Eine hohe Mauer und ein Tor schützen den Garten und seine Besucher vor vorwitzigen Blicken. Auf einem der Tische

ein kunstvolles Arrangement von Blumen und Früchten. • Un haut mur et un portillon en fer protègent le jardin du regard indiscret des curieux. Sur une table de jardin, fruits et fleurs forment une nature morte charmante.

PP. 190–191 Life in the depths of Provence provides pleasure for all the senses. This mouth-watering 'pissaladière' is a veritable feast for the eyes! • Im Herzen der Provence lässt es sich gut leben. Die von der Köchin Maury gebackene Pissaladière sieht gut aus und schmeckt auch so. • La vie est douce au cœur de la Provence et la pissaladière préparée par la cuisinière Maury un régal pour les yeux.

↑ The French window of the small drawing room opens out directly onto the shaded terrace. • Durch eine Fenstertür betritt man die schattige Terrasse. • La porte-fenêtre du petit salon donne directement sur la terrasse ombragée.

→ On the steps that lead to the garden and the swimming pool, a pair of stone Medici urns and a profusion of oleander catch the eye. • Auf dem Weg über die Freitreppe zu Garten und Schwimmbad stößt man auf ein Paar steinerner Medici-Vasen und üppig wuchernden

Oleander. • En empruntant le perron qui donne accès au jardin et à la piscine, le regard est attiré par une paire de vases Médicis en pierre et une profusion de lauriers-roses.

↑ A marble statuette dating from 1925. • Eine Marmorstatuette aus der Zeit um 1925. • Une statuette en marbre d'époque 1925.

→ In the entrance hall, a pair of 19th-century candelabra decorate a carved stone table. • Zwei Kandelaber aus dem 19. Jahrhundert zieren einen großen Steintisch am Eingang. • Dans l'entrée, une paire de candélabres 19ᵉ agrémentent une grande table de pierre.

← Lisa Kessel has installed an old stone sink under a side window, accentuating the simple, rustic feel of the kitchen. • Unter dem kleinen Fenster ließ die Hausherrin eine alte Steinspüle einbauen, die den rustikalen Charakter der Küche unterstreicht. • Près d'une petite fenêtre, la décoratrice a installé un évier en pierre ancien qui fait écho à l'aspect rustique de la cuisine.

↑ The kitchen was converted in style, retaining many of its original features. Beams and flagstone floors give the room a rustic, romantic feel. • Die vorhandenen Elemente der Küche wurden belassen, um eine romantisch-rustikale Atmosphäre zu schaffen. • La cuisine a été aménagée en respectant les éléments anciens pour créer une ambiance à la fois rustique et romantique.

↑ The elegant silhouette of the wrought-iron banister is accentuated by the simplicity of the monochrome staircase. • Das monochrome Treppen-haus lässt die elegante Silhouette des Geländers gut zur Geltung kommen. • La cage d'escalier monochrome met en valeur la silhouette élégante de la rampe en fer forgée.

→ The lady of the house's bed-room is infused with romantic tones. Lisa Kessel has brought her interior deco-rating skills to bear, juxtaposing 19th-century cast-iron chairs and agilt-framed mirror above the Baroque fireplace. • Das romantische Schlafzimmer der Hausherrin. Lisa Kessel kombinierte raffinierte gusseiserne Stühle aus dem

19. Jahrhundert mit einem goldge-rahmten Spiegel über dem barock geschwungenen Kamin. • La chambre romantique de la maîtresse de maison. La décoratrice Lisa Kessel a su marier des chaises de jardin 19ᵉ en fonte, un miroir à cadre doré et une cheminée aux formes baroques.

PP. 200–201 A fin-de-siècle ambience reigns in the conservatory, just off the master bedroom. The room is furnished with an elegant chaise-longue, a painted dressing screen and wrought-iron plantholders. • Im Wintergarten neben dem großen Schlafzimmer beschwören ein Diwan, zierliche Blumenständer und ein Paravent mit diversen Tier- und Pflanzenmotiven das Fin de Siècle herauf. • Ambiance fin de siècle pour la serre située près de la chambre maîtresse, grâce au lit de repos, aux jardinières et au paravent qui réunissent les éléments de la flore et de la faune.

← The bath adds an ostentatious edge, proving that a bathroom can be decorative as well as practical. • Die Badewanne zwischen Wandvertäfelungen im Directoire-Stil beweist, dass ein Bad nicht nur praktisch, sondern auch repräsentativ sein kann. • La baignoire entourée de boiseries dans le goût Directoire prouve que la salle de bains peut aussi devenir salon et chambre d'apparat.

↑ Romantic Belle Epoque style dominates in this guestroom where a 1900 beauty languishes beneath the bed's draped canopy. • Eines der Gästezimmer ist im Stil der Belle Epoque romantisch gestaltet. Unter dem Lambrequin lockt eine Schönheit von 1900. • Dans une chambre d'amis le ton est au romantisme Belle Époque. Sous un baldaquin une beauté 1900 attire le regard.

LA MAISON ROQUE

LA MAISON ROQUE
GÉRARD DROUILLET
EYGALIÈRES

The painter and ceramic artist Gérard Drouillet left this world far too soon, in 2011. All those who knew him have a lively memory of his Roman-emperor physique and his art, which was full of symbols that were violent and poetic at the same time. Born in Marseille, and with a gentleness that comes from living "at the bottom of the sea", he carved out a promising career for himself as a painter, but after meeting the antiquarian Bernard Paul – a dealer gifted with an exceptional eye – he joined him at l'Isle-sur-la-Sorgue, where Bernard had established the famous Espace Béchard. After the tragic disappearance of his companion, Gérard decided to stay on, at La Maison Roque, an old silkworm nursery dating from the 16th century. With his new partner, Frédéric Gigue, he continued to honour Paul's memory by surrounding himself with important examples of 20th-century design and pictures that carry his signature.

Der Maler und Keramiker Gérard Drouillet ist im Jahr 2011 viel zu früh verstorben. Wer ihn kannte, erinnert sich an seine Statur: Er sah aus wie ein römischer Kaiser, und seine Gemälde sind aufgeladen mit einer poetischen und heftigen Symbolsprache. Geboren in Marseille, war er geprägt vom „sanften Leben am Rande des Meeres" und machte sich früh einen Namen als vielversprechender Maler. Doch nachdem er den Antiquitätenhändler Bernard Paul kennenlernte, tat er sich mit diesem zusammen. Bernard Paul hatte einen scharfen Blick für Qualität und leitete schon seit langer Zeit auf der Insel Isle-sur-la-Sorgue den berühmten Espace Béchard für Antiquäten und Kunsthandwerk. Nach dem tragischen Tod seines Partners zog sich Gérard Drouillet in die Maison Roque zurück, eine ehemalige Seidenraupenzucht aus dem 16. Jahrhundert. Zusammen mit seinem neuen Partner Frédéric Gigue hat er hier eine Sammlung von wichtigen Designerstücken des 20. Jahrhunderts zusammengetragen.

Le peintre et céramiste Gérard Drouillet nous a quité beaucoup trop tôt, en 2011. Tous ceux qui l'ont connu se souviennent de son physique d'empereur Romain et de sa peinture pleine de symboles à la fois violents et poétiques. Né à Marseille, marqué par la douceur de vivre « en fond de mer » il s'était taillé une carrière de peintre prometteuse. Mais après avoir rencontré l'antiquaire Bernard Paul, un marchand doté d'un œil exceptionnel, il s'était installé à l'Isle-sur-la-Sorgue où Bernard avait créé le célèbre Espace Béchard. Après la disparition tragique de son compagnon, Gérard avait décidé de rester à La Maison Roque, une ancienne magnanerie datant du 16ᵉ siècle et avec son nouveau partenaire Frédéric Gigue il continua à honorer la mémoire de Paul en s'entourant de pièces majeures du design du 20ᵉ siècle et des tableaux qui portent sa signature.

PP. 204–205 Working in his tall, light-filled studio, Gérard Drouillet has put the finishing touch to an abstract triptych. • In dem hohen, lichterfüllten Atelier steht ein Triptychon, das Gérard Drouillet noch vollenden konnte. • Dans son atelier haut et clair, Gérard Drouillet venait de terminer un tableau en forme de triptyque.

P. 207 In a corner of the atelier, Gérard installed a table and a Scandinavian chair from the 1950s. He loved to draw here, and here he worked on his sculpture projects. • In einer Ecke seines Ateliers hatte Gérard einen Tisch und einen Stuhl aufgestellt – skandinavische Möbel aus den 1950er-Jahren. Hier zeichnete er gern und arbeitete an sei-

nen Skulptur-Projekten. • Dans un coin de l'atelier, Gérard avait installé une table et une chaise scandinave datant des années 1950. C'est ici qu'il aimait dessiner et qu'il travaillait sur les projets de ses sculptures.

← In the living room, Drouillet proves the truth of the Oscar Wilde maxim that "all beautiful things belong to the same age". A group of African statuettes and pieces of 1950s pottery are juxtaposed with a 40s baroque chair, an elegant lamp and a 50s sideboard. • Im Wohnraum belegt Drouillet Oscar Wildes Hypothese: „Alle schönen Dinge gehören derselben Zeit an." Die afrikanischen Statuetten und die Keramiken aus den 1950er-Jahren vertragen sich gut mit

Lampe und Anrichte aus derselben Zeit sowie einem barock geschwungenen Sessel aus den Vierzigern. • Dans le séjour, Drouillet prouve la véracité de la maxime « toutes les belles choses appartiennent à la même époque », signée Oscar Wilde. Ici les statuettes africaines et des faïences « fifties » cohabitent paisiblement avec un siège 1940 baroque, une lampe et une armoire-buffet des années 50.

↑ Gérard was sensitive to the allure of minimalism. The dining room bears no trace of ostentation. • Gérard bevorzugte schnörkellose Linien, im Esszimmer regiert edle Schlichtheit. • Gérard était sensible au design épuré. Rien d'ostentatoire dans la salle à manger.

↑ Drouillet was passionate about wood, in all aspects and forms. Here, an African stool sits next to an 18th-century 'banquette' while, to the left, a De Stijl-inspired chair is juxtaposed with a rustic wooden table. • Drouillet liebte Holz in jeder Erscheinungsform: Hier sind es ein afrikanischer Schemel und eine Bank aus dem 18. Jahrhundert. Links ein an De Stijl orientierter Stuhl neben einem rustikalen Tisch. • Drouillet aimait le bois, quel que soit son aspect et sous

toutes ses formes. Ici un tabouret africain côtoie une banquette 18ᵉ. À gauche, une chaise inspirée par De Stijl tient compagnie à une table rustique.

→ Architecture plays a prominent role in this converted silk farm. Restoring the building's original beams and wooden floors, the owner has decorated the interior with designer furniture from the 1950s, a pair of 1900 vases, and a group of elegant desklamps. • In der

einstigen Seidenraupenzucht spielt die Architektur die Hauptrolle. Die authentischen Holzdecken und -böden kombinierte der Hausherr mit Objekten der 1950er-Jahre, Vasen um 1900 sowie einfachen Schreibtischlampen. • Dans cette ancienne magnanerie, l'architecture joue un rôle majeur. Entre poutres et planchers d'époque, le maître de maison avait juxtaposé des créations des années 1950 et des lampes de bureau anonymes.

← Immaculate white walls dominate in the bathroom. A black-lacquered straw-bottomed chair, a veritable gem of 1950s design, is elegantly silhouetted against a stark white wall. • Im Bad dominiert makelloses Weiß, doch vor einer glatten, schmucklosen Wand hebt sich elegant die zierliche Silhouette eines schwarzen Stuhls mit Geflecht aus den 1950er-Jahren ab. • Dominée par un blanc immaculé, la salle de bains abrite néanmoins une chaise 1950 paillée et laquée noir dont la silhouette frêle et élégante se détache sur un pan de mur dépouillé.

↑ The simple graphic lines of designer furniture and the harmony of form and volume turn every corner into a subtle collage. • Nüchtern-geradlinige Designermöbel, Harmonie zwischen Raum und Formen – jeder Winkel dieses Hauses scheint subtil komponiert. • Graphisme sobre des meubles design, harmonie entre formes et volumes, chaque coin de la maison dénote un assemblage subtil.

213

JAS DE L'ANGE

JAS DE L'ANGE
ÉRIC & LAURENCE HANNOUN
ORGON

A few years ago on this spot, there was nothing but a vast pine forest and the ruins of an old silkworm farm where scrub and undergrowth had grown wild. Éric and Laurence Hannoun, a Parisian couple with a passion for the south of France, were not to be put off, however. The Hannouns were intent on finding their own sun-filled corner of Provence and building the house of their dreams. With the help of architect Hugues Bosc and the finest craftsmen in the region, the couple set about building their home using the farm's original stonework. Showing extraordinary courage and tenacity in the face of technical difficulties such as levelling the ground, the Hannouns supervised the long and meticulous construction of their 'mas' (Provençal farmhouse). Their old-world-style abode is full of rustic charm with its blue shutters, trailing roses, quaint vegetable patch and its magnificent garden filled with olive trees and the heady scent of lavender. Éric and Laurence have now opened Jas de l'Ange as a guest house, inviting visitors to share the comfort and tranquillity of their idyll, where exotic touches such as a Mauritanian tent blend perfectly with the spirit of Provence.

Hier fanden Éric und Laurence Hannoun einst nur einen großen Pinienhain und die überwucherten Ruinen einer alten Seidenraupenzucht. Doch davon ließen sich die beiden keineswegs abschrecken. Schon seit Langem suchten die gebürtigen Pariser in ihrer geliebten Provence nach einem sonnigen Plätzchen für ihr künftiges Traumhaus. Aus den Resten der verfallenen „magnanerie" erbauten sie es nun mithilfe des Architekten Hugues Bosc und der geschicktesten Handwerker der Region. Mit Mut und Beharrlichkeit meisterten die Hannouns alle Probleme, von der Nivellierung des Terrains bis zum langwierigen Bau selbst. Dank ihrer archäologischen Liebe zum Detail entstand mit dem Jas de l'Ange ein stilechtes provenzalisches „mas" von faszinierendem Charme. Das Haus mit seinen blauen Fensterläden und Kletterrosen, dem umfriedeten Küchengarten und dem Park mit seinen Olivenbäumen, in dem es so herrlich nach Lavendel duftet, wurde schon bald ein Gasthaus im besten Sinne: Gemeinsam mit Éric und Laurence genießen die Besucher den Komfort und die ruhige Lage des Hauses. Exotische Accessoires wie das mauretanische Zelt bilden die perfekte Ergänzung zum markanten Charme der Provence.

À l'origine, il n'y avait qu'une vaste pinède et les ruines d'une ancienne magnanerie envahie par les broussailles. Mais il en fallait bien plus pour décourager Éric et Laurence Hannoun, Parisiens d'origine et amoureux du Midi, depuis toujours à la recherche d'un coin de Provence ensoleillé et de la maison de leurs rêves. Cette maison, ils la construisirent en utilisant les pierres de la magnanerie, avec l'aide de l'architecte Hugues Bosc et des meilleurs artisans de la région. Ce qui étonne aujourd'hui, c'est le courage et la ténacité des Hannoun qui ont été confrontés à une montagne de difficultés comme le nivellement du sol et la construction lente et méticuleuse du « mas », exécutée avec une patience d'archéologue, pour aboutir à la création d'une bâtisse trompeusement ancienne au charme fou. Baptisée Jas de l'Ange, la maison rustique aux volets bleus, dotée de rosiers grimpants, d'un potager clos et d'un jardin ouvert planté d'oliviers et qui embaume la lavande devint bientôt maison d'hôtes. Éric et Laurence partagent avec leurs hôtes le confort et le silence des lieux, une surprenante tente mauritanienne et de petites touches exotiques qui se marient à merveille avec l'âme de la Provence.

PP. 214–215 The owners have erected a Mauritanian tent in the courtyard, adding an exotic note to their typically Provençal dwelling. • Vor dem typisch provenzalischen Haus errichteten die Besitzer ein mauretanisches Zelt, dessen Fremdheit in diesem Umfeld ins Auge sticht. • Devant la maison typiquement provençale, les propriétaires ont dressé une tente mauritanienne. Le dépaysement est garanti cent pour cent !

P. 217 The Jas de l'Ange may be a recent addition to the landscape, but it blends in perfectly with the centuries-old houses in the region. • Das erst vor wenigen Jahren gebaute Jas de l'Ange unterscheidet sich in keiner Weise von den authentischen Profanbauten der Region. • Le Jas de l'Ange, construit il y a quelques années, ressemble à s'y méprendre aux bâtiments séculaires qui font la fierté de la région.

← A climbing rose twines its stem around the skeleton of a dead tree, accentuating the wild beauty of the Provençal landscape. • Eine Kletterrose erobert einen toten Baum: ein Sinnbild der spröden Schönheit provenzalischer Landschaft. • Un arbre mort envahi par un rosier grimpant accentue la beauté sauvage du paysage provençal.

↑ A wrought-iron bed stands in the shade of a tree, the mosquito net draped from an overhanging branch flapping in the gusts of the Mistral. • Ein schmiedeeisernes Bett im Schatten von Bäumen. Das Moskitonetz hängt von einem Ast herab und bläht sich unter den Böen des Mistral. • Un lit en fer forgé à l'ombre d'un arbre. La moustiquaire accrochée à l'une des branches se bat contre les bourrasques du Mistral.

← A colourful lounge area behind the main door welcomes guests from around the world. The lanterns bathe the setting in magical Oriental light by night. · Nahe der Eingangstür lädt eine gemütliche Ecke Gäste aus der ganzen Welt zum Verweilen ein. Laternen verströmen ein geheimnisvoll orientalisches Licht. · Près de la porte d'entrée un coin repos accueille les hôtes venus du monde entier. Les lanternes évoquent les soirées magiques teintées d'Orient.

↑ Provençal flavours mingle with North African spices beneath the tapering lid of a tajine. · Wer sagt, eine Tajine könne die Gewürze Afrikas nicht mit den Aromen der Provence paaren? · Qui prétend que les saveurs de Provence et les épices africaines ne peuvent cohabiter dans le tajine ?

PP. 222–223 Secluded behind high stone walls and shaded by overhanging greenery, the terrace makes an ideal spot for al fresco dining. · Mit ihren hohen Mauern und der schattigen Pergola, die sich darüberspannt, ist die Terrasse ein ideales Plätzchen für Mahlzeiten im Freien. · La terrasse, entourée de hauts murs et ombragée par une tonnelle, est le lieu rêvé pour des repas à la fraîche.

↑ A romantic lacquered white bed, an elegant canopy of fine gauze curtains set off against pale lemon walls: three perfect reasons to linger at the Jas de l'Ange. · Ein Baldachin aus durchscheinenden Vorhängen, ein weiß lackiertes romantisches Bett und zitronengelbe Wände – drei gute Gründe für ein paar Tage im Jas de l'Ange. · Un baldaquin drapé de rideaux diaphanes, un lit romantique laqué blanc et des murs jaune citron : trois raisons pour passer quelques jours au Jas de l'Ange.

↓ A lacquered yellow wardrobe stands against a backdrop of vibrant yellow walls. A geranium-red lampshade picks up a vermilion stripe on the bedcover. The Midi sun appears to have stimulated the decorators, inspiring them to use a bold colour scheme. • Ein knallgelb lackierter Schrank, leuchtend gelbe Wände und ein Lampenschirm im Geranienrot der Streifen der Tagesdecke:

Die südfranzösische Sonne muss den Innenausstatter zu solch kühnen Nuancen inspiriert haben. • L'armoire laquée jaune vif, les murs d'un jaune vibrant et l'abat-jour qui fait écho au rouge géranium du couvre-lit rayé prouvent que le soleil du Midi a stimulé la palette des décorateurs et leur a inspiré une gamme audacieuse.

JOHN BURNINGHAM & HELEN OXENBURY

JOHN BURNINGHAM &
HELEN OXENBURY
DRÔME PROVENÇALE

It is impossible to cite the names John Burningham and Helen Oxenbury in anything other than one breath, for these two artists appear to be linked by an invisible umbilical cord. Over the years, Burningham and Oxenbury have established an international reputation as book illustrators. Few are those who, as children, did not pore over Helen's charming drawings in "We're Going on a Bear Hunt" or laughed themselves close to tears turning the pages of "John Burningham's France", John's mischievously funny portrait of the country both he and Helen adore. Not surprisingly, the couple's French home, which the Burningham-Oxenburys admit they spent a small fortune on restoring, echoes their personalities. John and Helen fell in love with the ruined country house nestling at the foot of Mont Ventoux, but it took great audacity and a vivid imagination to transform an old Provençal farm into a Tuscan villa. The couple boldly added a balcony, an 18th-century tower, new floors, a Hollywood-style pool and a loggia worthy of a Roman villa.

Die Namen John Burningham und Helen Oxenbury getrennt zu nennen erscheint geradezu unmöglich, so eng sind die beiden Künstler einander verbunden. Beide sind Buchillustratoren, und ihr überragendes Talent ist weltweit ein Begriff. Wer von uns hat nicht als Kind das von Helen illustrierte Buch „Wir gehen auf Bärenjagd" gelesen oder Tränen über „John Burningham's France" gelacht, eine augenzwinkernde Hommage an das Land, das John und Helen so sehr lieben? Ihr Haus ist Spiegel ihrer Seele. Für die Restaurierung einer Ruine am Fuß des Mont Ventoux haben die beiden zugegebenermaßen ein Vermögen ausgegeben. Es gehört schon viel Mut und Ideenreichtum dazu, ein provenzalisches Landhaus in eine toskanische Villa zu verwandeln, komplett mit neuem Balkon, einem Turm aus dem 18. Jahrhundert, neuen Dielenböden, einem Schwimmbecken und einer Loggia, die jedes römische Haus zieren würden.

Impossible de mentionner les noms de John Burningham et Helen Oxenbury séparément, tant il semble que ces artistes soient liés par un cordon ombilical invisible. Burningham et Oxenbury sont des illustrateurs de livres, et leur grand talent est reconnu dans le monde entier. Tout le monde ou presque a lu dans son enfance « La chasse à l'ours » – illustré par Helen – et ri aux larmes en parcourant les pages de la « France » de John Burningham, un portrait plein d'humour et de malice d'un pays que John et Helen adorent. Et la maison qu'ils y possèdent fait écho à leur personnalité. Les Burningham-Oxenbury avouent qu'ils ont dépensé une somme ridicule pour restaurer une maison de campagne en ruine au pied du Mont Ventoux. Il faut de l'audace et de l'inventivité pour transformer une grande ferme provençale en villa toscane en y ajoutant un balcon, une tour 18e des planchers neufs, une piscine hollywoodienne et une loggia digne d'une villa romaine.

PP. 226–227 Behind the house, the vineyard stretches away to the horizon bathed in a soft, Provençal glow reminiscent of Tuscany. • Hinter dem Haus erstrecken sich endlose Weingärten. Die Provence erscheint hier in den Farben der Toskana. • Des vignes s'étendent à perte de vue derrière la maison. Ici la Provence emprunte les couleurs de la Toscane.

P. 229 Next to the pool, Helen and John have built an 18th-century-style pavilion. • Neben dem Schwimmbecken ließen Helen und John ein Häuschen im

Stil des 18. Jahrhunderts errichten. • Près de la piscine, Helen et John ont fait construire un pavillon 18ᵉ trompeusement authentique..

← An embroidered Art Deco cushion draws the eye to an elegant three-seater sofa upholstered in damask. The mirror gives the room an added sense of depth. • Ein Stickkissen im Art-Déco-Stil lenkt den Blick auf die mit feinem Damast bezogene große Couch. Der Spiegel täuscht Raumtiefe vor. • Un coussin brodé typiquement Art Déco se love dans le vaste canapé houssé

d'un tissu damassé. Le grand miroir donne une illusion de profondeur.

↑ The living-room, converted from a former barn, features an eye-catching staircase whose clear, vertical lines strikingly contrast with the rounded forms of this antique terracotta pot. • In der alten Scheune, dem heutigen Wohnraum, kontrastiert die geradlinige Treppe mit einer bauchigen alten Terrakottavase. • Dans l'ancienne grange transformée en séjour, l'escalier aux lignes épurées contraste avec les rondeurs d'un pot en terre cuite ancien.

← The masters of the house indulge their eclectic taste for decor, juxtaposing a magnificent refectory table with a pot from Les Anduzes and a Victorian armchair. In winter, a cosy logfire roars in the vast stone hearth. • Ein massiver Refektoriumstisch, ein Anduze-Topf und ein viktorianischer Sessel belegen den eklektischen Geschmack der Hausbesitzer. Im Winter sorgt der riesige offene Kamin für behagliche Wärme. • Une magnifique table de réfectoire, un pot des Anduzes et un fauteuil victorien révèlent le goût éclectique des maîtres de maison. En hiver, la grande cheminée répand une chaleur réconfortante.

LA BASTIDE DE MARIE

LA BASTIDE DE MARIE
MÉNERBES

To have a centuries-old house with its own vineyard in one of the most beautiful parts of France, in reach of charming villages, has been a dream of many. High in the Lubéron Mountains of Provence, that fantasy can come a little true by staying at La Bastide de Marie, a small inn more like a home than a hotel. Set in a vineyard that produces promising red, white, and rosé Côtes du Lubéron, the rustic old farmhouse has been given a new lease of life. Contemporary restful colours, and the peace and quiet of the setting make this a haven for travellers who crave tranquillity and nourishment of body and mind. When the air is scented with lavender, sunlight bathes the walled garden, and delectable food and wine are served beside the pool, one could dream of not going home. On a nearby hillside is the picturesque village of Ménerbes. This may be as far as guests of La Bastide de Marie might want to venture. For those who feel like going further on shopping expeditions, there are lively weekly markets in the surrounding countryside, specialising in collectables from pottery to antiques.

Wer hat nicht schon einmal davon geträumt, Besitzer eines jahrhundertealten Hauses mit eigenem Weinberg zu sein, welches in einer der schönsten Regionen Frankreichs liegt, umgeben von charmanten Dörfern? Zumindest für eine Weile können Sie sich diesen Traum hoch in den Lubéron-Bergen der Provence in La Bastide de Marie erfüllen, einem bezaubernden kleinen Hotel, das fast wie ein Zuhause ist. Inmitten eines Weinbergs gelegen, der vielversprechenden roten, weißen und rosé Côtes du Lubéron hervorbringt, erlebt dieses rustikale alte Bauernhaus einen zweiten Frühling. Angenehme, ruhige Farben und die friedliche Umgebung machen es zu einer Zuflucht für Reisende, die sich nach stressfreier Erholung für Körper und Seele sehnen. Wenn Lavendelduft in der Luft liegt, die Sonne auf dem von Mauern geschützten Garten liegt und am Pool köstliche Gerichte und Weine serviert werden, lässt es sich leicht davon träumen, für immer zu bleiben. Auf einem nahe gelegenen Hügel liegt das malerische Dörfchen Ménerbes. Und weiter möchten sich viele Gäste von La Bastide de Marie möglicherweise gar nicht entfernen. Wer aber gern auch mal einen Einkaufsbummel unternimmt, sollte die lebhaften Wochenmärkte in den Dörfern der Umgebung besuchen, wo Sammlerstücke von Töpferwaren bis zu Antiquitäten angeboten werden.

Nombreux sont ceux qui rêvent de posséder une vieille maison nichée au cœur des vignes, non loin de charmants villages, dans l'une de ces belles régions de France. Ce rêve se réalise le temps d'un séjour à La Bastide de Marie, une petite auberge perchée dans les Montagnes du Lubéron, qui évoque davantage une maison de famille qu'un hôtel. Située dans un vignoble produisant d'excellents Côtes du Lubéron rouges, blancs et rosés, cette ancienne ferme a trouvé une nouvelle jeunesse. Le décor aux couleurs reposantes et le cadre serein en font un havre de paix pour qui a soif de quiétude et recherche à la fois des nourritures spirituelles et terrestres. Séduit par l'air embaumant la lavande, par le soleil qui baigne le jardin clos et par les mets et vins délicieux servis près de la piscine, on s'imaginerait bien de ne plus jamais rentrer chez soi. Sur une colline voisine s'élève le pittoresque village de Ménerbes. Parfois, les hôtes de La Bastide de Marie ne souhaitent pas s'aventurer plus loin. Les marchés hebdomadaires des environs offrent toutes sortes d'objets, des faïences aux antiquités.

PP. 234–235 Provence – that means lavender! In the walled garden of La Bastide de Marie, a bed of lavender fills the air with its captivating perfume. • Provence und Lavendel gehören zusammen! Im von Mauern umgebenen Garten der Bastide de Marie verströmt ein Lavendelbeet seinen hinreißenden Duft. • Qui dit Provence dit lavande et dans le jardin clos de murs de La Bastide de Marie un parterre de lavande embaume l'air avec son parfum captif.

P. 237 The table is set for lunch, and from the terrace you have a commanding view of a landscape bathed in sunlight. • Die Tische auf der Terrasse sind für die Mittagsmahlzeit gedeckt, mit unbezahlbarem Blick auf eine von der Sonne durchflutete Landschaft. • La table est mise pour le déjeuner et de la terrasse on a une vue imprenable sur le paysage inondé de soleil.

↑ The three-level swimming pool is surrounded by cypress trees and extends towards the verdant Lubéron hills. • Das Schwimmbad auf drei Ebenen ist von Zypressen umgeben. Die Bäder sind in Richtung der blühenden Hügel des Lubéron angelegt. • La piscine à trois niveaux s'entoure de cyprès et s'étend en direction des collines verdoyantes du Lubéron.

→ It feels so good to rest on one of the sun loungers lined up beside the swimming pool and to take a siesta under a traditional wicker awning with a glass of rosé to hand ... • Es ist einfach nur wohltuend, sich auf den Liegen entlang der Becken auszustrecken, ein feines Glas Rosé in Reichweite, beschirmt von einem Sonnenschutz aus Korbgeflecht. • Il fait bon se reposer sur les transats qui s'alignent le long de la piscine et de faire la sieste dans l'ombre d'un auvent traditionnel en corde avec un verre de rosé à portée de la main...

↑ Laid out in front of the house, the terrace is equipped with wrought iron tables and chairs, and offers guests the comfort of a shady corner. • Eine Terrasse liegt direkt am Hauseingang. Sie ist mit Tischen und Stühlen aus Eisenwerk ausgestattet und bietet den Gästen einen schattigen Ort der Ruhe. • Installée devant la maison, la terrasse a été équipée avec des tables et des chaises en fer forgé et elle offre à ses hôtes le confort d'un coin ombragé.

→ In Provence, it's second nature to protect yourself from the midday sun. To provide shade for farmhouse guests eating their lunch, the owners have set up an ample awning. • In der Provence muss man sich mittags schon vor der starken Sonne schützen. Die Gastgeber in La Bastide haben eine großzügige Laube errichtet, damit ihre Gäste die Mahlzeiten im Schatten einnehmen können. • En Provence, on se protège d'office du soleil de midi et pour que les hôtes de la bastide puissent prendre leur repas à l'ombre on a crée un auvent aux proportions généreuses.

← Beneath the vaulted ceiling of the dining room, the Louis XVI-style medallion chairs are lined up either side of an old, rustical refectory table. • Unter den Gewölben des Speisesaals umgeben Stühle im Louis-XVI-Stil einen langen ehemaligen Refektoriumstisch. • Sous les voûtes de la salle à manger des chaises médaillon de style Louis XVI se rangent le long d'une ancienne table de réfectoire rustique.

↑ Above the grey-painted, country-style chest, the owners have hung a charming scene of Provençal life. • Auf der bäuerlichen Kommode, die grau gestrichen wurde, findet man hier ein apartes Gemälde mit einer ländlichen Szene aus der Provence. • Au-dessus de la commode campagnarde peinte en gris, on a posé un tableau représentant une charmante scène de la vie provençale.

← A pair of gilt and Murano-glass standing candelabras of the 1940s make a surprising contrast to the rustical decoration of the sitting room. • Ein Paar Kerzenständer aus den 1940er-Jahren, aus Muranoglas und vergoldetem Metall, kontrastiert erfrischend mit der rustikalen Einrichtung des Zimmers. • Une paire de candélabres « années 40 » en

métal doré et verre de Murano forme un contraste surprenant avec la décoration rustique du séjour.

↑ In front of the bookcase, which is full of old books and various decorative objects, a pair of cane loungers seem to be turning their backs on the lower part of the sitting room. • Vor einem Regal, das

mit antiquarischen Büchern und Sammelstücken gefüllt ist, kann man in zwei Rohrstuhl-Liegen dem tiefer gelegenen Teil des Zimmers den Rücken zukehren. • Devant la bibliothèque remplie de livres anciens et d'objets divers, une paire de transats cannées donne l'impression de tourner le dos à la partie basse du séjour.

← It resembles a grotto, this beautiful, vaulted bedroom, painted white throughout. One can imagine that it feels deliciously cool within its thick walls. • Dieses Zimmer mit seiner Gewölbedecke erinnert an eine Höhle. Mit seinen weiß gestrichenen Wänden wirkt es trotz der dicken Steine freundlich und frisch. • Elle ressemble à une grotte, cette belle chambre voûtée peinte en blanc et on s'imagine qu'il fait délicieusement frais entre ses murs épais.

↑ The sleek form of this wrought iron four-poster bed, draped with curtains, is inspired by the Provençal beds of the 18th century. The furniture and the objects that complete the decoration have been chosen with the same wish for simplicity. • Das edle Himmelbett aus Schmiedeeisen mit schweren Vorhängen ist von den historischen Betten der Provence inspiriert. Die anderen Möbel und Einrichtungsgegenstände sind mit der gleichen Sorgfalt und dem Blick

für das Wesentliche ausgesucht. • La forme épurée d'un lit à baldaquin en fer forgé drapé de rideaux s'inspire des lits provençaux d'époque 18e. Les meubles et les objets qui complètent la décoration ont été choisis avec le même souci de simplicité.

UNE MAISON
TROGLODYTE

UNE MAISON TROGLODYTE
MÉNERBES

Provence is full of picturesque villages, perched atop rocky hillsides, which add their singular beauty to the overall charm of the region. Ménerbes is one of these magical spots which, in the past, has drawn famous figures such as Dora Maar and Nicolas de Staël, and continues to attract artists and lovers of old stone. One day a French antique dealer roamed Ménerbes's labyrinthine streets and alleyways, lined with small Provençal houses and sumptuous residences, but decided to make his home in a troglodyte dwelling, partially built into the rockface. The house, made up of a multitude of tiny rooms whose forms curve up the steep incline of the hill, has a magnificent vaulted living-room carved directly into the rock which provides a cool and refreshing refuge in the summer months. Impressed by this truly unique setting, the new owner has transformed the stunning troglodyte dwelling into a backdrop for his vast collection of religious antiques. Set off by typical Provençal colours and period furniture, statues of Christ and the Virgin rub shoulders with angels and an amazing assortment of crucifixes, accentuating the charm and old-fashioned beauty of this exceptional spot.

Die Provence ist unglaublich reich an malerischen Dörfern, die wie i-Tüpfelchen über der wunderschönen Landschaft hoch oben auf felsigen Hängen thronen. Eines dieser bildhübschen Städtchen ist Ménerbes. Auf den Spuren berühmter Leute wie Dora Maar oder Nicolas de Staël fühlen sich Künstler und Liebhaber alter Gemäuer gleichermaßen angezogen von den märchenhaft verschlungenen Straßen und den von kleinen Häusern und stattlichen Palästen gesäumten Gassen. Ein ortsansässiger Antiquitätenhändler wählte als seinen Wohnsitz in Ménerbes eine Art Höhlenhaus, das teilweise in den Hang hineingebaut ist. Die Anordnung der zahlreichen kleinen Räume folgt genau der steil abfallenden Böschung. Unmittelbar in den Felsen geschlagen wurde ein überwölbter Raum, der auch in der Hitze des Sommers erfrischend kühl bleibt. Betört von dieser einzigartigen Konstellation beschloss der neue Besitzer, das Haus eigne sich ideal für seine umfangreiche Sammlung sakraler Objekte. Inmitten typisch provenzalischer Farben und geschmackvoller alter Möbel bilden Madonnen, Christusstatuen, Engel und Kruzifixe unterschiedlicher Stile und Epochen ein ausgefallenes Ensemble von herrlich altmodischem Charme.

La Provence possède un véritable trésor de villages pittoresques, lesquels, perchés au sommet de collines rocheuses, semblent vouloir couronner ce magnifique pays de leur beauté singulière. Ménerbes ne fait pas exception à la règle et, suivant l'exemple de célébrités comme Dora Maar et Nicolas de Staël, des artistes et amateurs de vieilles pierres se sont sentis attirés par la magie de ses rues labyrinthiques et de ses ruelles bordées de petites maisons et de palais imposants. L'antiquaire qui s'est établi à Ménerbes a choisi une habitation troglodyte, construite partiellement dans le rocher. Composée d'une multitude de pièces aux dimensions modestes dont la disposition suit étroitement la pente raide de la colline, la maison possède une salle voûtée, creusée dans la masse rocheuse, qui peut servir de frais salon d'été. Séduit par cette demeure unique en son genre, notre antiquaire a décidé qu'elle servirait d'écrin à sa vaste collection d'objets religieux. Sur fond de couleurs provençales et soutenus par la présence de beaux meubles anciens, les Vierges, les Christ, les anges et les crucifix d'époques et de styles divers accentuent la beauté et le charme désuet de ce lieu hors du commun.

PP. 248–249 You reach the hermit-age along a narrow lane that leads up to the Ménerbes hills. The residents couldn't resist the temptation to brighten up the entrance with a little garden. • Die Einsiedelei erreicht man nur über eine schmale Straße, die hinauf nach Ménerbes führt. Die Besitzer konnten der Versuchung nicht widerstehen, die Besucher mit einem kleinen Garten zu empfangen. • On atteint la maison troglodyte en empruntant un chemin étroit qui monte vers les hauteurs de Ménerbes. Les habitants n'ont pas pu résister à la tentation d'égayer l'accès avec un jardinet.

P. 251 On the terrace side, the door is crowned by the abundant foliage of an old wisteria tree. On these back steps, topiary evergreen balls stand sentinel. • Die vielen Äste einer alten Glyzinie be-schirmen die Terrassentür, und die Trep-pen werden von rund geschnittenen Buchsbäumen bewacht. • Côté ter-rasse la porte d'entrée se coiffe avec la végétation abondante d'une vieille gly-cine. Sur les marches du perron des buis taillés en boule jouent les sentinelles.

← A collection of religious objects assembled on a window sill makes a dra-matic still life. • Auf der Fensterbank wurde ein Stillleben aus sakralen Objekten arrangiert. • Sur l'appui d'une fenêtre, une nature morte composée de quelques objets religieux.

↑ The vaulted grotto is a treasure trove of 18th-century antiques and rustic furni-ture. Visitors are always fascinated by the pink gravel floor. • Das Höhlenhaus quillt über von Antiquitäten des 18. Jahr-hunderts und rustikalen Möbeln. Der rosa Kiesboden verblüfft immer wieder Besucher. • La grotte voûtée foisonne d'antiquités 18ᵉ et de meubles rustiques. Son sol en gravier rose ne manque pas de surprendre les visiteurs.

P. 254 An 18th-century painted wooden statuette of the Christ Child is haloed in natural light. • Tageslicht fällt auf ein geschnitztes Jesuskind aus polychromem Holz aus dem 18. Jahrhundert. • Un bois sculpté polychrome du 18ᵉ siècle représentant l'Enfant Jésus capte la lumière du jour.

P. 255 A 19th-century drape decorated with the image of a saint hangs in the stairway. • Im Treppenhaus hängt eine Kirchenfahne mit Heiligendarstellung aus dem 19. Jahrhundert. • Une ban-

nière 19ᵉ ornée d'une image sainte a été accrochée dans la cage d'escalier.

↑ The master of the house is an avid collector of antique fabrics, which came in handy for decorating the guestroom. • Als begeisterter Sammler alter Stoffe hatte der Hausherr keine Mühe, das Bett in diesem Gästezimmer stilvoll zu beziehen. • Grand collectionneur de tissus anciens, le maître de maison n'a pas eu à faire trop d'efforts pour habiller le lit dans une chambre d'amis.

→ The cave is decorated with 18th-century furniture, antique benches and rustic stools. A collection of Provençal devotional objects adds a religious touch. • Das Gewölbe wurde ausgestattet mit Möbeln aus dem 18. Jahrhundert, rustikalen Bänken und Schemeln sowie einer Sammlung provenzalischer Devotionalien. • La grotte a été décorée avec un mobilier d'époque 18ᵉ, des bancs, des tabourets rustiques et une collection d'objets de piété provençaux.

LA GRANDE BÉGUDE

LA GRANDE BÉGUDE

JULIETTE & FRANÇOIS LOCHON
GOULT

There are some magical places in this world which merely need to be woken from their slumbers. La Grande Bégude is one of these. The old coach inn, built in 1622, lies deep in the heart of the Lubéron, near an ancient Roman road, in the midst of picturesque countryside irrigated by the river Calavon. One day, a couple of wayfarers crossed its courtyard and mounted the ancient stone staircase. It would take all the audacity of photo-reporter François Lochon and his partner Juliette's passion for decor to efface the ravages wreaked by time and the elements. The couple say the restoration process appeared interminably long as they strove to maintain the building's soul and preserve the original patina of its stonework and the sobriety of its architecture. The giant plane tree in the garden must certainly recall the Lochons' relentless onslaught and the multitude of local craftsmen who lent their skills day after day. The result is a magnificent guest house which exudes the warmth of a Provençal summer's afternoon and offers guests the charm of ancient beams, vaulted ceilings, antique furniture, romantic bathrooms and wonderfully big comfy beds.

Es gibt Orte, die geradezu danach „schreien", wachgeküsst zu werden. Dazu gehörte wohl auch die alte Poststation La Grande Bégude. Sie entstand 1622 an einer alten Römerstraße im Herzen des Lubéron, einer Landschaft, die dem Fluss Calavon ihre Fruchtbarkeit verdankt. Als eines Tages ein Ehepaar die Schwelle des Hauses überschritt, quer über den Hof ging und die weite, hellgelbe Steintreppe hinaufstieg, war es so weit. Ein forscher Reporter und seine Frau mit einem Faible für Dekoration machten sich daran, alle Spuren von Alter und Verwitterung zu tilgen. Juliette und François Lochon erinnern sich gut an die endlose Restaurierung: ihre Sorge, ob sie die Seele des Hauses, seine heimelige Stimmung, die Patina seines Steins und die schlichte Bauweise würden retten können. Auch die große Platane erinnert sich sicher an den zähen Kampf und die zahllosen Handwerker, die sich in einem fort die Klinke in die Hand gaben. Die Mühe hat sich gelohnt: Das Gebäude verströmt den warmherzigen Charme eines Sommertags in der Provence und bezaubert mit seinen mächtigen Balken, den Deckengewölben, Stilmöbeln, romantischen Bädern und kuscheligen Betten.

Il est des lieux qui attendent d'être libérés de leur profond sommeil. La Grande Bégude, un ancien relais de poste construit en 1622, situé au cœur du Lubéron près d'une ancienne voie romaine au milieu d'une campagne irriguée par la source du Calavon, en fait partie. Un jour, un couple a franchi le seuil, traversé la cour et gravi le grand escalier en pierre blonde. Il fallait un photoreporter audacieux et sa compagne passionnée par la décoration pour lutter contre les effets de l'âge et les ravages dus aux éléments. Juliette et François Lochon se souviennent d'une restauration qui leur a semblé interminable. Ils racontent leur souci de préserver l'âme de la maison, son ambiance accueillante, la patine de sa pierre et la sobriété de son architecture. Le grand platane se souvient sans doute de leur lutte acharnée et du passage d'une multitude d'artisans pour créer une maison d'hôtes chaude comme une fin de journée d'été provençal. La demeure offre le charme de ses poutres anciennes, de ses plafonds voûtés, de ses meubles classiques, de ses salles de bains romantiques et de ses grands lits douillets.

PP. 258–259 The old plane tree, which has stood in the middle of the courtyard for over a century, spreads its branches above a long banquet table where guests gather to share a pastis aperitif, a meal or a simple chat. • Unter der alten Platane, die seit über hundert Jahren mitten im Hof steht, treffen sich die Gäste am langen Tisch zu einer Mahlzeit, einem Gläschen Pastis oder einfach einem gemütlichen Schwatz. • Sous le vieux platane qui se dresse depuis plus d'un siècle au milieu de la cour, les hôtes peuvent se réunir autour d'une longue table, le temps d'un repas, d'un verre de pastis ou d'un papotage convivial.

P. 261 The old coaching inn is secluded behind a high stone wall, which protects guests' privacy. • Eine hohe Mauer umgibt die ehemalige Poststation und schützt die Gäste vor aufdringlichen Blicken. • Un haut mur entoure l'ancien relais de poste et protège les hôtes des regards indiscrets.

↑ Following a very old tradition, a suitor has used his penknife to carve his polite declaration of love onto a tree trunk. • Wie es die Tradition will, hat ein Verehrer mit seinem Taschenmesser eine Liebeserklärung an diesem Baumstamm hinterlassen. • Fidèle à une très vieille

tradition, un soupirant s'est servi de son canif pour tailler sa déclaration d'amour dans l'écorce d'un arbre.

→ This wall fountain is framed by a vine branch. Someone has just filled an old zinc watering can. • Der Wandbrunnen wird von einer Weinranke eingefasst. Die Zinkkanne ist gerade mit Wasser gefüllt worden, und nun geht es ans Gießen der Pflanzen. • La fontaine murale est entourée d'une branche de vigne et on vient de remplir un vieil arrosoir en zinc qui servira à arroser les plantes.

↑ In this ballroom-sized suite on the first floor, a set of imposing wooden beams provide a loft canopy for the rococo bed. Furniture is kept to a minimum in the bedroom to emphasise the beauty of the room's volumes. • Ein offener Dachstuhl als Baldachin über dem Rokoko-Bett. Das Schlafzimmer im ersten Stock ist groß wie ein Ballsaal, jedoch nur sparsam möbliert, um den Raum an sich zur Geltung zu bringen. • Une charpente imposante sert de baldaquin à un lit rococo dans une suite à l'étage. Grande comme une salle de bal, la chambre à coucher a été meublée sobrement pour mettre en valeur la beauté du volume.

→ On the first floor landing, the austere architecture is broken by two simple decorative details: a garden bench and an old-fashioned rocking horse. • Auf dem Treppenabsatz im ersten Stock beleben nur eine Gartenbank und ein Schaukelpferd die ansonsten völlig schmucklose Architektur. • Sur le palier du premier étage, un banc de jardin et un cheval à bascule sont la seule note décorative dans cette architecture austère.

PP. 266–267 A refined and peaceful atmosphere reigns beneath the vaulted ceiling of the vast living room, where wing chairs and period furniture are silhouetted in sunlight filtering through the tall curtains. • Unter der Gewölbedecke des Salons schufen die Eigentümer ein behagliches Ambiente. Durch die Vorhänge gedämpft, umschmeichelt das Sonnenlicht die bequemen Polstersessel und das klassische Mobiliar. • Sous les voûtes du vaste salon, les propriétaires ont créé une ambiance feutrée. Les rideaux filtrent le soleil et la lumière sculpte la silhouette des bergères et du mobilier aux lignes classiques.

JEAN & DOROTHÉE
D'ORGEVAL

JEAN & DOROTHÉE D'ORGEVAL
ROUSSILLON

Jean and Dorothée d'Orgeval's home began life as a simple farmhouse and pigsty. Coming across this rustic abode, hidden away in a shady alleyway in the heart of Roussillon, the couple of antique dealers instantly recognised its potential and set about transforming it into a sophisticated and elegant holiday home. Among the house's most striking features are the warm ochre tones of the walls. Roussillon is internationally famous for its rich red earth, and the d'Orgevals took advantage of the local colour, mixing the pigment with their whitewash. Arriving in the garden, visitors will discover that the house, perched high on a hill, is surrounded by rocks whose rugged red hues echo the rich palette in the house's interior. The d'Orgevals' decor provides a perfect backdrop to the sturdy Provençal furniture, as well as to a magnificent Louis XIII couch and a sumptuous bed from the same period hung with a Hungarian-point tapestry are complimented by an impressive collection of faïences from Apt. The lady of the house was responsible for the stunning trompe-l'œil frescos in the bathroom and is equally famous for the succulent feasts she cooks up on the grill.

Gut versteckt im Schatten einer Gasse mitten in Roussillon stand einst ein großer Bauernhof mit Schweinestall. Jean und Dorothée d'Orgeval, Antiquitätenhändler, fanden ihn so imponierend, dass sie das rustikale Anwesen in ein Wohnhaus von raffinierter Eleganz verwandelten. Wer die Schwelle zu ihrem Ferienhaus heute überschreitet, ist angenehm überrascht vom warmen Ockerton der Wände. Das Pigment für die Kalkfarbe fanden beide in der rötlich gelben Erde, für die Roussillon weltweit berühmt ist. Ihr Haus steht auf einer Hügelkuppe, und vom Garten aus blickt man ringsum auf Felsen, deren Töne der schillernden Farbpalette der Hausbesitzer in nichts nachstehen. Wände und Böden bilden einen geglückten Rahmen für das prächtige Louis-XIII-Kanapee, in der Ecke des Salons das Prunkbett aus derselben Epoche mit besticktem Behang und extravaganten Federbüschen, dazu eine beachtliche Sammlung von Fayencen aus Apt. Die Trompe-l'Œil-Fresken im Bad stammen von der Hausherrin selbst – ebenso wie die Köstlichkeiten vom Grill.

À l'origine, c'était une grande ferme avec porcherie cachée à l'ombre d'une ruelle au cœur de Roussillon. Les antiquaires Jean et Dorothée d'Orgeval lui ont trouvé si fière allure qu'ils n'ont pas hésité à transformer cette demeure rustique en une maison élégante et raffinée. Poussant la porte de leur maison de vacances, le visiteur est agréablement surpris par le ton ocre des murs. Roussillon, mondialement célèbre pour sa terre rousse, a fourni à Jean et Dorothée le pigment qu'ils ont mélangé à la chaux. En se dirigeant vers le jardin, on découvre que la maison, située au sommet d'une colline, est entourée de rochers qui font écho à la palette chatoyante des maîtres de maison. Le décor se marie à merveille avec le mobilier robuste, typiquement provençal et avec un magnifique canapé Louis XIII, un lit d'apparat de la même époque habillé d'une tapisserie au point de Hongrie, qui occupe un coin du séjour, de frivoles panaches et une collection impressionnante de faïences d'Apt. C'est à la maîtresse de maison qu'on doit les fresques en trompe-l'œil dans la salle de bains ainsi que les repas succulents préparés sur le gril.

PP. 268–269 A Louis XIII four-poster bed, decorated with plumes, occupies a place of honour in the living room. The room is, in fact, multi-functional, being a place where Jean and Dorothée can dine, sleep and entertain. • Das Wohnzimmer dominiert ein Louis-XIII-Himmelbett mit Federbuschaufsätzen. Der multifunktionale Raum dient Jean und Dorothée als Schlaf-, Ess- und Empfangszimmer zugleich. • Un lit à baldaquin d'époque Louis XIII garni de panaches trône dans le séjour. La salle est multifonctionnelle, car c'est ici que Jean et Dorothée dorment, dînent et reçoivent leurs amis.

← and P. 271 The d'Orgevals lunch "al fresco" at a massive stone table in the garden. For intimate dinners indoors they relocate to a rustic wooden table in the living room set with wrought-iron chairs. • Ihre Mahlzeiten nehmen die d'Orgevals entweder am großen Steintisch im Garten oder im gemütlichen Wohnzimmer an einem rustikalen Tisch mit schmiedeeisernen Stühlen ein. • Les d'Orgeval prennent leurs repas sur une grande table de pierre au jardin ou dînent en toute intimité dans le séjour sur une table rustique entourée de chaises en fer forgé.

↑ An alcove in the living room doubles as a display cabinet, exhibiting the d'Orgevals' impressive collection of Provençal pottery from the 18th and 19th centuries. • In einer Wohnzimmernische fand die ansehnliche Sammlung provenzalischer Fayencen aus dem 18. und 19. Jahrhundert ihren Platz. • Dans une niche du séjour, les d'Orgeval ont trouvé l'endroit idéal pour exposer leur belle collection de faïences provençales du 18e et du 19e siècle.

PP. 274–275 A traditional logfire blazes in the massive stone hearth. Spring evenings in Provence can often be chilly. • Im offenen Kamin knistert und knackt ein behagliches Feuer, denn die Frühlingsabende in der Provence sind oft frisch. • Un grand feu de bois crépite dans l'âtre de la vaste cheminée. En Provence, les soirées de printemps sont souvent fraîches.

↑ Snuggle up in the heart of Roussillon in this magnificent four-poster bed hung with ochre-coloured drapes whose colour is picked up on the matching quilt. The 'prie-dieu' beside the bed is a fine example of 18th-century cabinet-making. • Es ist herrlich, in Roussillon unter einem ockerfarbenen Betthimmel und einem gleichfarbigen Steppbett aufzuwachen. Das Betpult links stammt aus dem 18. Jahrhundert. • Il fait bon se réveiller au cœur du Roussillon dans un lit à baldaquin drapé d'un tissu ocre recouvert d'un « piqué » de la même couleur. Le prie-Dieu à gauche est d'époque 18ᵉ.

→ A bouquet of dried branches artfully arranged in an antique vase makes a striking cornerpiece. • Ein paar Zweige genügen, um aus einer schönen, klassisch geformten Vase ein Stillleben zu gestalten. • Quelques branches esquissent une nature morte dans un joli vase aux formes classiques.

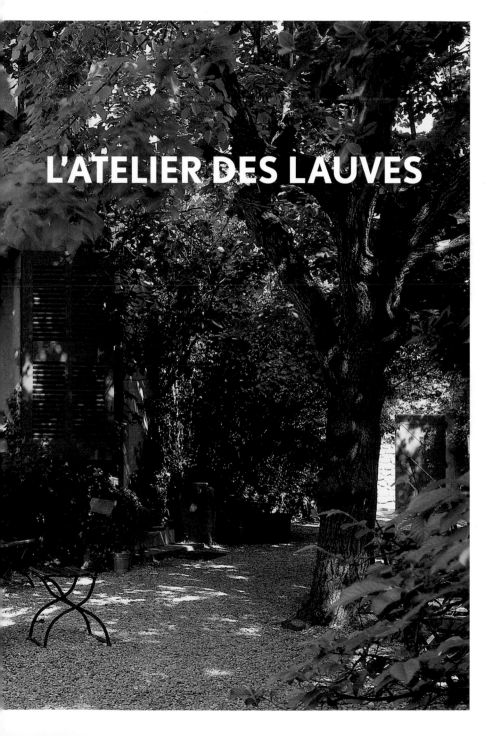

L'ATELIER DES LAUVES

L'ATELIER DES LAUVES

PAUL CÉZANNE
AIX-EN-PROVENCE

"Young Marie has just been in to clean my studio. It's finished now and I'm moving in bit by bit," Cézanne wrote to his niece, Paule Conil, on 1 September 1902. The grand master of Aix could finally paint in peace and quiet, shut away in his spacious 'atelier' on the upper floor of a modest country house. It was here on the outskirts of Aix, in his studio on the Chemin des Lauves, that the painter came to create his unique artistic universe dominated by still lifes of his favourite accessories: bottles, a plaster statue of Cupid, an assortment of human skulls and that famous earthenware bowl full of apples. It was here that he painted his superb "Bathers", laying the canvas flat on the floor and peering down at it from the top of a ladder to inspect progress. Cézanne died in Aix, in his apartment on the Rue Boulegon, on 22 October 1906, and silence descended on the studio where he had once dreamt of "conquering Paris with an apple". It was the writer Marcel Provence who saved the studio and its contents for posterity. And it was thanks to an American project master-minded by the late John Rewald that the Lauves studio finally opened its doors to Cézanne fans in 1954.

„Die kleine Marie hat mein Atelier geputzt, das nun fertig ist und in dem ich mich nach und nach einrichte", schrieb Cézanne am 1. September 1902 an seine Nichte Paule Conil. Endlich hatte der Künstler Ruhe zum Malen in seiner geräumigen Werkstatt im obersten Stock eines Landhauses. Im Atelier am Chemin des Lauves schuf er sein Universum, insbesondere die Stillleben mit seinen liebsten Accessoires – Flaschen, ein Gips-Cupido, Totenköpfe und die unvermeidliche Fayenceschale mit Äpfeln. Hier entstanden auch die „Badenden": Seine Fortschritte prüfte er von einer Leiter aus, während die Leinwand flach auf dem Boden lag. Als Cézanne am 22. Oktober 1906 in seiner Wohnung in der Rue Boulegon in Aix starb, wurde es still im Atelier des Mannes, der sich vorgenommen hatte, „Paris mit einem Apfel zu erobern". Dem Schriftsteller Marcel Provence verdanken wir, dass Atelier und Inhalt überdauerten. Durch eine amerikanische Initiative unter Leitung von John Rewald konnte das Atelier des Lauves 1954 seine Pforten wieder öffnen – für alle Cézanne-Verehrer und diejenigen, die einen Augenblick lang in sein magisches Universum eintauchen möchten.

«La petite Marie a nettoyé mon atelier qui est terminé et où je m'installe peu à peu», écrit Cézanne le 1er septembre 1902 à sa nièce Paule Conil. Le maître d'Aix peut maintenant peindre en toute tranquillité, dans un vaste atelier au sommet d'une modeste maison de campagne. Dans son atelier du chemin des Lauves, en bordure d'Aix, Cézanne va se construire un univers où domineront des natures mortes composées avec ses accessoires préférés – des bouteilles, un cupidon en plâtre, quelques crânes humains et l'incontournable coupe en faïence remplie de pommes. Il y créera ses sublimes «Baigneurs», inspectant du haut d'une échelle leur évolution sur la toile couchée à même le plancher. Cézanne meurt à Aix, le 22 octobre 1906 dans son appartement de la Rue Boulegon et le silence descend sur l'atelier de celui qui rêvait de «conquérir Paris avec une pomme». C'est à l'écrivain Marcel Provence que nous devons la survie de l'atelier et des objets. Et c'est grâce à une initiative américaine présidée par feu John Rewald que l'atelier des Lauves a ouvert ses portes en 1954 aux admirateurs de Cézanne et à tous ceux qui veulent, l'espace d'un moment, se plonger dans son univers magique.

PP. 278–279 Simple and stripped of all ornamentation, Cézanne's humble studio reflected the artist's need for solitude and silence. • Mit seiner bescheidenen, schmucklosen Atmosphäre erfüllte das Atelier Cézannes Bedürfnis nach Einsamkeit und Stille. • Modeste, dépouillé de tout ornement, l'atelier de Cézanne répondait parfaitement à son besoin de solitude et de silence.

P. 281 The door is always open to Cézanne enthusiasts who wish to spend a few moments in the place where the artist created so many of his masterpieces. • Die Tür ist stets offen für Bewunderer des Malers, die für ein paar Minuten an dem Ort verweilen möchten, an dem viele seiner Meisterwerke entstanden. • La porte est toujours ouverte aux admirateurs du peintre venus passer quelques instants à l'endroit où naquirent nombre de ses chefs-d'œuvre.

← The interior has been reconstructed with a painstaking eye to detail. Even the most ordinary corner of the room houses a still life which could have been composed by Cézanne himself. • Alles wurde mit erstaunlicher Präzision rekonstruiert. Noch die banalste Ecke äh-nelt einem Stillleben, wie es der Maler selbst hätte schaffen können. • Tout a été reconstruit avec une précision remarquable. Même le coin le plus banal nous offre l'image d'une nature morte que l'artiste aurait pu composer.

↑ Red shutters and pale lemon walls bathed in the golden sunlight of Provence. • Rote Fensterläden und hellgelbe Wände fangen das goldene Licht der provenzalischen Sonne ein. • Volets rouges et murs jaune pâle reflètent la lumière dorée du soleil de Provence.

↑ Cézanne's walking stick and the hat which the artist wore come rain, wind or shine, still hang in their customary places. • Cézannes Hut, getreuer Gefährte an Wind- und Regentagen, und sein Spazierstock, der ihn auf allen Wegen begleitete, befinden sich noch an Ort und Stelle. • Le chapeau de Cézanne, fidèle compagnon des jours de vent et de pluie, et la canne qui l'accompagnait lors de ses promenades sont toujours en place.

→ The tall wooden easel stands by the window with its back to the light.

The old cast-iron stove in the corner kept Cézanne warm through long winter days. • Die große Staffelei am Fenster steht mit dem Rücken zum Licht. Der gusseiserne Ofen wärmte den Maler an kalten Wintertagen. • Près de la fenêtre, le grand chevalet tourne le dos à la lumière. Le poêle en fonte a réchauffé le peintre pendant les froides journées d'hiver.

PP. 286–287 The Atelier des Lauves contains everything the artist needed to compose his famous still lifes. It is a moving experience walking round the studio and finding the fruitbowls, skulls, wine bottles and plaster cherub standing untouched. • Das Atelier am Chemin des Lauves enthält alles, was der Künstler für seine Stillleben benötigte. Bewegt erkennt der Besucher Schalen, Totenköpfe, Flaschen und den Gips-Cupido, die er auf seinen Bildern verewigte. • L'Atelier des Lauves renferme tout ce dont le peintre avait besoin pour composer ses natures mortes. On reconnaît avec émotion les coupes, les crânes, les bouteilles et le chérubin en plâtre qu'il a immortalisés sur ses toiles.

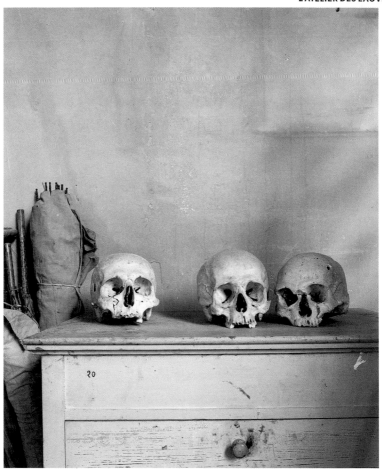

← The artist's palette, his paintbox and his wooden manikin lie in a corner near an 18th-century screen from his parents' house, Jas de Bouffan. • Palette, Malkasten und Gliederpuppe des Künstlers neben einem Paravent aus dem 18. Jahrhundert, der schon in seinem Elternhaus, dem Jas de Bouffan, stand. • Sa palette, sa boîte à couleurs, son mannequin articulé se languissent. Le paravent 18ᵉ vient de la maison de ses parents, le Jas de Bouffan.

↑ It is thanks to John Rewald's passion and admiration for Cézanne that this

magical place has survived intact. If it had not been for Rewald's dedication, and generous donations from American enthusiasts, the artist's studio would have fallen into ruin. • Der Bewunderung John Rewalds für Cézanne verdanken wir die genaue Rekonstruktion dieser magischen Stätte. Ohne seine Hingabe und die großzügigen Spenden vieler amerikanischer Verehrer wäre der Ort mit Sicherheit nicht so erhalten worden. • C'est à l'admiration et à la passion de John Rewald pour Cézanne que nous devons la reconstitution exacte de cet endroit magique. Sans son dévoue-

ment et sans les fonds généreux des nombreux admirateurs américains, il aurait connu un sort déplorable.

PP. 290−291 A still life of apples and onions, arranged in the folds of a tea towel, has been carefully reconstructed on the table. • Auf dem Tisch stellt man liebevoll Stillleben mit Äpfeln und Zwiebeln nach. Unverzichtbar: das in Falten gelegte Geschirrtuch. • Sur la table, on a reconstruit méticuleusement les natures mortes aux pommes et aux oignons, sans oublier les plis du torchon.

289

CHÂTEAU DE CASSIS

CHÂTEAU DE CASSIS
CASSIS

Once this castle above the limestone cliffs of Cassis belonged to the imperium of the Les Baux family – the legendary dynasty that, at its peak, exercised its mighty rule over almost 80 towns and villages in the region and had the castle converted into a fortress housing 250 residents. It is difficult to imagine so many people up here today: with just nine rooms, Château de Cassis is one of the most exclusive "chambres d'hôtes" in Provence – a guest house that eschews official hotel status and an endless list of services, instead offering an uncomplicated ambience and an individual design. During years of renovation work the young owner Chloé Caussin has, in all the right places, either erased or emphasised the marks left by history, and under the old vaulting mixes styles in a carefree manner: so it is that the "Suite Romantique" is fitted out with classic furniture and maintained in pastel shades, in the suite "La Tour" futuristic bedside tables, made of metal, will take guests by surprise, and the "Suite Marocaine" exudes Middle Eastern charm thanks to its warm colours, a four-poster bed and Moroccan accessories.

Einst gehörte dieses Anwesen über der Kalksteinküste von Cassis zum Imperium der Familie Les Baux – der legendären Dynastie, die auf dem Höhepunkt ihrer Macht über fast 80 Orte der Region herrschte und die Burg zu einer Festung für 250 Bewohner ausbauen ließ. So viele Menschen kann man sich hier oben heute kaum mehr vorstellen: Mit gerade einmal neun Zimmern ist das Château de Cassis eines der exklusivsten „Chambres d'Hôtes" der Provence – ein Gästehaus, das auf offiziellen Hotelstatus sowie eine Endlosliste von Services verzichtet und stattdessen unkompliziertes Ambiente sowie individuelles Design bietet. Die junge Besitzerin Chloé Caussin hat in jahrelanger Renovierungsarbeit die Spuren der Geschichte an den jeweils richtigen Stellen getilgt oder betont und mischt unter alten Gewölben unbeschwert die Stile: So ist die „Suite Romantique" mit klassischen Möbeln ausgestattet und in Pastell gehalten, in der Suite „La Tour" überraschen futuristische Nachtschränkchen aus Metall, und die „Suite Marocaine" verströmt dank warmer Farben, eines Himmelbetts und marokkanischer Accessoires orientalisches Flair.

Trônant majestueusement au-dessus des falaises de calcaire de Cassis, ce château faisait partie autrefois de l'empire de la famille des Baux, une dynastie légendaire, qui au plus fort de son pouvoir régna sur plus de 80 villages de la région et fit transformer le château en une forteresse accueillant 250 habitants. De nos jours, il est difficile d'imaginer autant de monde là-haut : avec ses neuf chambres, le château de Cassis est une des « chambres d'hôtes » les plus luxueuses de Provence. Il renonce au statut officiel d'hôtel ainsi qu'à une liste infinie de prestations et propose à la place une ambiance détendue et un design individuel. La jeune propriétaire Chloé Caussin a, durant de longues années de travaux de restauration, effacé ou accentué aux bons endroits les traces de l'histoire. Sous les vieux arcs voûtés, les styles sont mélangés avec audace : la suite romantique aux teintes pastel est aménagée de meubles classiques, la suite « La Tour » surprend avec ses petites tables de nuit futuristes en métal et des couleurs chaudes, le lit à baldaquin et les accessoires marocains confèrent à la suite marocaine un air oriental.

PP. 292–293 The Château de Cassis overlooks the port and the Bay of Cassis. From their terraces, the guests can enjoy a spectacular view of the sea. • Das Anwesen liegt oberhalb des Hafens und der Bucht von Cassis. Von den Terrassen aus hat man einen spektakulären Blick aufs Meer. • Le Château de Cassis surplombe le port et la baie de Cassis et de leurs terrasses les hôtes peuvent se régaler d'une vue spectaculaire sur la mer.

P. 295 The double wrought-iron gate – a true work of metalworking art – grants access to an adjoining terrace. • Durch dieses Tor aus Schmiedeeisen, ein Meisterwerk seiner Art, geht es zur nächsten Terrasse. • La double porte en fer forgé

– un véritable chef-d'œuvre de l'art de la ferronnerie – donne accès à une terrasse attenante.

← Constructed entirely in Cassis stone originating from the famous Cacau bunkers, the former fortress has four top-luxury suites. From their private terraces, guests have a panoramic view of the town. • Das Gebäude ist aus Cassis-Steinen aus dem berühmten Steinbruch in Cacau erbaut und bietet seinen Gästen vier luxuriöse Suiten. Jede hat eine eigene Terrasse mit Panorama-Blick auf die nahe gelegene Stadt. • Construite entièrement en pierre de Cassis provenant des célèbres trémies de la Cacau, le château possède quatre suites de

grand luxe. De leurs terrasses individuelles les hôtes ont une vue imprenable sur le panorama de la ville.

↑ The medieval appearance of the stout square tower gives no indication of the discreet luxury of the suites located inside the building. • Mittelalterlich wirkt der stämmige viereckige Turm und gibt keinen Hinweis auf den diskreten Luxus der einzelnen Suiten, die sich hinter den Mauern verbergen. • L'aspect médiéval de la robuste tour carrée ne donne aucun indice sur le luxe discret des suites qui se trouvent à l'intérieur de la bâtisse.

↑ Safe from prying eyes, the large pool is hidden behind high walls that date from the time of the Carolingian Empire. • Der Pool ist vor indiskreten Blicken geschützt. Das große Becken liegt hinter hohen Mauern, die ihrerseits noch aus der Zeit der Karolinger stammen. • Protégée des regards indiscrets, le grand bassin de la piscine se cache derrière des hauts murs qui, eux, datent du temps de l'Empire Carolingien.

→ The swimming pool is situated among greenery. It's surrounded by fine, tall specimens of the cypress tree – an icon for van Gogh and symbolic for everyone who holds Provence dear. • Das Schwimmbecken ist von gepflegten Gärten und schlanken Zypressen umgeben. Diese Bäume galten van Gogh als Inbegriff der Provence, und das sind sie auch heute noch für alle, die diese Landschaft lieben. • La piscine s'entoure d'un espace verdoyant planté de hauts cyprès : l'arbre fétiche de Van Gogh et de tous ceux qui portent la Provence dans le cœur.

↑ Why not linger in the coolness, sit down for a moment at the edge of the water and rest in the shade of an old tree's crooked branches? • Warum auch nicht im Freien verweilen, sich an den Rand des Wassers setzen und sich im Schatten des alten Baumes mit seinen gewundenen Zweigen ausruhen? • Pourquoi ne pas s'attarder dans la

fraîcheur, s'asseoir un moment sur le rebord de la pièce d'eau et se reposer à l'ombre d'un vieil arbre aux branches tortueuses ?

→ This view of a high stone wall and a dilapidated, wooden, half-open gate excite our curiosity and we can well ask ourselves what is hidden behind it... •

Ein Blick auf diese hohe Steinmauer und das heruntergekommene halb offene Holztor daneben weckt unsere Neugier – was mag sich wohl dahinter verbergen? • La vue d'un haut mur en pierres et d'une porte en bois vermoulue excite la curiosité et on a bien le droit de se demander ce qui se cache au-delà du mur...

↑ Under the majestic vaulted ceiling of the former fortress, the stone walls bear witness to the turbulent past of the Château de Cassis; yet no-one can remain indifferent to the story of its spectacular revival. • Unter den majestätischen Gewölben der ehemaligen Festung erzählen die steinernen Mauern von der bewegten Vergangenheit des Château de Cassis, aber auch die spektakuläre Wiedergeburt des Gebäudes lässt niemanden unberührt. • Sous les voûtes majestueuses de l'ancien château fort,

les murs en pierre racontent le passé mouvementé du Château de Cassis et le récit de sa résurrection spectaculaire ne laissera personne indifférent.

→ An elegant ensemble of Louis XV-style wing chairs takes care of the guests' comfort. We can't fail to notice that the colours of the upholstery reflect the blackcurrant and sunflower tones typical of the region. • Ein elegantes Arrangement von Bergère-Sesseln im Louis-XV-Stil sorgt für den Komfort der Gäste.

Und wir bemerken, dass sich in den Bezugsstoffen die typischen Brombeer- und Sonnenblumenfarben der Region wiederfinden. • Un ensemble élégant composé de « bergères » de style Louis XV se charge du confort des hôtes. Les couleurs du revêtement n'échappent pas à la comparaison avec les tons « Cassis » et « Tournesol » typiques pour la région.

↑ A sunny patio embellished with a classical colonnade enables the guests in this suite to fully enjoy the gentle Provençal climate. · Den sonnigen Innenhof umgibt ein klassischer Wandelgang mit Säulen. So lässt sich das milde Klima der Provence am besten genießen. · Un patio ensoleillé agrémenté d'une colonnade classique permet aux

hôtes de cette suite de profiter pleinement du doux climat provençal.

→ When the evenings become cooler, you just have to light a large wood fire. The limestone chimney dates from the 18th century. · Wenn die Abende kühler werden, muss nur ein Feuer im Kamin angezündet werden. Der Kamin aus

Kalkstein stammt aus dem 18. Jahrhundert. · Quand les soirées se font plus fraîches, on allume un grand feu de bois. La cheminée en pierre calcaire date du 18ᵉ siècle.

PP. 306–307 The stone walls and floors guarantee absolute coolness in the rooms. In Provence the sun reigns but we don't like it to sneak inside! • Steinerne Wände und Fußböden sorgen für angenehme Frische in den Räumen. In der Provence mag zwar die Sonne regieren, aber hier lassen wir sie nicht herein! • Les murs et des sols en pierre garantissent une fraîcheur absolue dans les chambres. En Provence le soleil est roi mais on n'aime pas qu'il essaye de se faufiler à l'intérieur !

← An exotic atmosphere pervades this suite with its walls of red ochre. The Moroccan lantern and the Anglo-Indian four-poster bed accentuate the impression of being in a far-away country. • In dieser Suite findet man sich in einer exotischen Atmosphäre, mit ockerfarbenen Wänden, einer marokkanischen Lampe und einem Himmelbett aus dem Indien der Kolonialzeit. So fühlt man sich wie in einem fernen Land. • Une ambiance exotique règne dans cette suite aux murs peints en ocre rouge. La lanterne marocaine et le lit à baldaquin anglo-

indien accentuent l'impression de se trouver dans un pays lointain.

↑ The red-brick fireplace and the walls of terracotta red imbue the interior with the atmosphere of a riad. • Der Kamin aus roten Ziegelsteinen und die terrakottafarbenen Wände erinnern an ein Haus im traditionellen marokkanischen Riad-Stil. • La cheminée en briques rouges et les murs couleur terre cuite rappellent la décoration traditionnelle des riads marocains.

PP. 310–311 At Château de Cassis, the suite decoration is notable for the total absence of fake luxury. The immaculately white walls and the simple, pure lines of the furniture deliberately avoid flashy effects. • Die Einrichtung der Suiten im Château de Cassis zeichnet sich durch den wohltuenden Verzicht auf jeglichen falschen Luxus aus. Die reinen weißen Wände und das schlichte Mobiliar verweigern sich aufdringlichen Effekten. • Au Château de Cassis, la décoration des suites se distingue par l'absence totale du faux luxe. Les murs

d'un blanc immaculé et le mobilier aux lignes épurées s'éloignent volontairement des effets « tape à l'œil ».

↑ It's all in the detail: on a rough stone windowsill the guest will discover some woven cotton towels and a slab of Savon de Marseille soap. • Alles steckt im Detail: Auf dem Fenstersims aus grob bearbeitetem Stein liegen ein baumwollenes Handtuch und ein Stück „savon de Marseille" bereit, traditionelle Seife aus Olivenöl. • Tout est dans le détail : sur un appui de fenêtre en pierre rugueuse,

on découvre un essuie-mains en coton tissé et un cube de Savon de Marseille.

→ A clever choice of materials and accessories has transformed this basic bathroom into a delightful space. • Klug gewählte Ausstattung und schöne Materialien machen aus diesem einfachen Badezimmer eine wahre Augenweide. • Le choix des matériaux et des accessoires transforment cette salle de bains minimale en un véritable plaisir pour les yeux.

FRÉDÉRIC MÉCHICHE

FRÉDÉRIC MÉCHICHE
HYÈRES

Those who know Frédéric Méchiche well, know his unpredictable about-turns in decorating matters, because unexpectedly the 18th-century style risks giving way to 1940s style, and this will next be pitilessly dethroned by the minimalism of vintage design! In purchasing an old fisherman's house in one of the narrow streets of Vieux Hyères, the designer took on the difficult task of artificially ageing a house that was already several centuries old. He added patinas and ravages of time in a trompe l'oeil effect, selected furniture for its aged appearance and created the illusion of a window on the past... And then: what a dramatic turn of events! From one day to the next the Directoire-style furniture and Toiles de Jouy fabrics were replaced by discoveries with the stamp of Harry Bertoia or Verner Panton, and artificially old sheens were covered with a thick layer of white paint. "That's also Provence!" cried Méchiche, and who dared to contradict him?

Wer Frédéric Méchiche nur ein wenig kennt, rechnet immer mit Überraschungen: in seiner Inneneinrichtung lösen plötzlich die Vierzigerjahre das 18. Jahrhundert ab, nur um ihrerseits von minimalistischem Vintage-Design entthront zu werden! Das ehemalige Haus eines Fischers in einer der engen Gassen der Altstadt von Hyères ist bereits einige Jahrhunderte alt, und der Designer hat es mithilfe von künstlicher Patina und Trompe-l'Œil-Effekten noch weiter altern lassen. Dazu wählte er Möbel, die besonders „verlebt" aussahen, um das Fenster in die Vergangenheit weit zu öffnen. Und dann eine vollständige Kehrtwende: die Möbel des Directoire und Toile-de-Jouy-Stoffe mussten neu entdeckten Designerstücken von Harry Bertoia und Verner Panton weichen. Die altertümliche Patina wurde mit dickem Weiß überstrichen „Auch das ist die Provence!", erklärt Méchiche, und wer wollte ihm widersprechen?

Ceux qui connaissent bien Frédéric Méchiche connaissent ses volte-face imprévisibles en matière de décoration car sans crier gare le style dix-huitième risque de céder la place au style années quarante et ce dernier sera ensuite détrôné sans pitié par le minimalisme du design vintage ! En achetant une ancienne maison de pêcheur dans une des ruelles étroites du Vieux Hyères, le décorateur entreprit la tâche difficile de vieillir une maison déjà vielle de plusieurs siècles. Il ajouta des patines et des « ravages du temps » en trompe-l'œil, choisit des meubles pour leur aspect « vécu » et obtint l'illusion d'une fenêtre sur le passé... Et puis : coup de théâtre ! D'un jour à l'autre les meubles Directoire et les Toiles de Jouy furent remplacés par des trouvailles signés Harry Bertoia et Verner Panton et les patines anciennes artificielles se couvrirent d'une couche épaisse de peinture blanche. « Ca aussi, c'est la Provence ! » s'écrie Méchiche et qui oserait le contredire.

PP. 314–315 Frédéric Méchiche decided to part with his previous decor,
replacing the 18th-century ambience
with the black-and-white look of the
'60s and the designs of Verner Panton
(1926-1998). · Frédéric Méchiche
hat sich entschieden, seinem vorange-
gangenen Dekor Adieu zu sagen, und
das Ambiente des 18. Jahrhunderts
durch einen Schwarz-Weiß-Look der
Sechzigerjahre und Designerstücke
von Verner Patton (1926-1998) zu
ersetzen. · Frédéric Méchiche avait
décidé de dire adieu à sa décoration
précédente et de remplacer l'ambiance
dix-huitième par le look noir et blanc
des « sixties » et des créations de Verner
Panton (1926-1998).

P. 317 Back when his house had an
18th-century look, the walls of the
entrance hall were painted blue and
Frédéric had kept the old terracotta
tiles and the dilapidated front door. ·
Frédéric hat Teile des ehemaligen
Dekors des 18. Jahrhunderts belassen,
so die blauen Wände der Eingangs-
halle und die Terrakottafliesen und
sogar die wurmstichige Eingangstür. ·
Du temps de l'ambiance dix-huitième
les murs de l'entrée avaient été peint
en bleu et Frédéric avait gardé le sol
en tomettes anciennes et la porte vermoulue de l'entrée.

← In what was previously a bedroom,
the designer had installed his living
room. The original details had been
preserved and his furniture and old collector's pieces completed the deceptive
period decor. · Was einmal ein Schlafzimmer war, hat der Designer in sein
Wohnzimmer verwandelt. Originale
Details wurden belassen, Möbel und
Sammelstücke komplettieren die Illusion
der Vergangenheit. · Dans ce qui était
jadis une chambre à coucher, le décorateur avait installé son séjour. Les détails
originaux avaient été préservés et ses
meubles et des objets anciens complé-
taient le décor trompeusement
d'époque.

P. 319 In a niche, a silhouette portrait and porcelain dishes of the period were chosen for their strict black-and-white colour scheme. • In einer Nische findet sich ein Porträt im Scherenschnitt, dazu gesellt sich altes Porzellan, das wegen seines strengen schwarz-weißen Dekors ausgewählt wurde. • Dans une niche, un portrait-médaillon en « silhouette » et une vaisselle en porcelaine d'époque avaient été choisis pour leur décor rigoureusement blanc et noir.

↑ Frédéric brushed the walls with a bluish wash and each item was chosen for its authenticity. • Frédéric hat hier die Wände mit einem leichten Blauton versehen und davor einige ausgewählte Gegenstände versammelt. • Frédéric avait badigeonné les murs avec un lavis bleuâtre et chaque objet avait été choisi pour son authenticité.

→ The kitchen walls are adorned with antique cake tins. The green tiles are typical of the region. • Die Küchenwand ist mit alten Backformen geschmückt. Die grünen Fliesen sind typisch für die Region. • Des moules à gâteau anciens ornent les murs de la cuisine. Les carrelages verts sont typiques de cette région.

320

→ The 18th-century tiled floor in the living room is genuine, but the walls and ceiling bear the signature of the owner. The pedestal table and the faience urn date from the early 19th century. • Der Steinboden ist aus dem 18. Jahrhundert, während Decke und Wände die Hand des Hausherrn verraten. Beistelltisch und Wasserbehälter aus Keramik stammen aus dem frühen 19. Jahrhundert. • Dans le séjour, le sol en tomettes du 18e siècle est authentique mais le plafond et les murs portent la signature du maître de maison. La table-guéridon et la citerne en faïence sont début 19e siècle.

↑ In a corner of the room the whiteness of a Directoire armchair contrasts with the black concept for the furniture and the objects surrounding it. · In einer Ecke des Raumes kontrastiert ein weißer Directoire-Sessel mit dem Schwarz der übrigen Möbel und Objekte. · Dans un coin de la chambre la blancheur d'un fauteuil Directoire contraste avec le graphisme noir des meubles et des objets qui l'entourent.

→ At one time, you really thought that you were back in the 18th century. Every corner of the house was a window onto the past. · Man glaubt sich im 18. Jahrhundert, und in jeder Ecke des Hauses öffnet sich ein Fenster in die Vergangenheit. · On se croyait vraiment au 18e siècle et chaque coin de la maison devenait une fenêtre sur le passé.

PP. 326–327 The living room is on the top floor and in this crooked little room, Méchiche has created the perfect illusion of period decor. The Louis XVI wing arm-chair has a plain linen cover and the Directoire mirror reflects the room's only window. • Das Wohnzimmer liegt im ersten Stock. In diesem eher kleinen, ungewöhnlich geschnittenen Raum ist Méchiche die Rückkehr in die Vergangenheit perfekt gelungen. Der gepolsterte Louis-XVI-Lehnstuhl wurde mit einfachem Leinen bezogen, während der Directoire-Spiegel das einzige

Fenster verdoppelt. • Le séjour se trouve au dernier étage, et dans cette pièce biscornue aux dimensions modestes, Méchiche a créé l'illusion parfaite d'un décor d'époque. La bergère Louis XVI est recouverte d'une simple toile de lin et le miroir Directoire reflète l'unique fenêtre.

↑ Frédéric took great pleasure in composing still lifes that resembled paintings. • Frédéric hat mit viel Vergnügen Stillleben geschaffen, die an Gemälde erinnern. • Frédéric s'était donné à

cœur joie en composant des natures mortes qui ressemblaient à des tableaux.

→ A water tank of Provençal faience and a Directoire chair form a simple and harmonious composition. • Ein Wasserbehälter aus provenzalischer Fayence und ein Directoire-Stuhl bilden ein schlichtes und harmonisches Ensemble. • Un réservoir à eau en faïence provençal et une chaise Directoire formaient un ensemble simple et harmonieux.

↑ Whiteness compels, and the bedroom, stripped of its former decor, has become a room in the minimalist style. • Hier hat das Weiß die Oberhand gewonnen, und das Schlafzimmer, von seinem alten Dekor befreit, ist ein minimalistisches Kunstwerk. • Blancheur oblige et la chambre à coucher s'est dépouillée de son ancienne décoration et est devenu une pièce minimaliste.

→ The staircase has not been modernised in any way. The charm of its whitewashed walls and uneven steps has survived intact. • Die Treppe wurde nicht aufgearbeitet, sondern durfte den Charme ihrer unregelmäßigen Stufen vor weiß gekalkten Wänden bewahren. • L'escalier n'a pas subi de cure de jouvence et a gardé le charme de ses murs blanchis à la chaux et de ses marches irrégulières.

← The metamorphosis of the bedroom is impressive. A contemporary work of art accentuates the modernity of the decor. · Die gelungene Metamorphose des Schlafzimmers ist beeindruckend. Ein zeitgenössisches Kunstwerk akzentuiert die Modernität der Einrichtung. · La métamorphose de la chambre à coucher est impressionnante et une œuvre d'art contemporaine accentue la modernité du décor.

↑ In the guesthouse, Méchiche has gone for a timeless minimalist look based on a simple black-and-white colour scheme. · Bei dem kleinen Gästehaus entschied sich Méchine für zeitlose Schlichtheit in Schwarz und Weiß. · Pour la petite maison d'amis, Méchiche jugea la palette blanc et noir et la sobriété intemporelle.

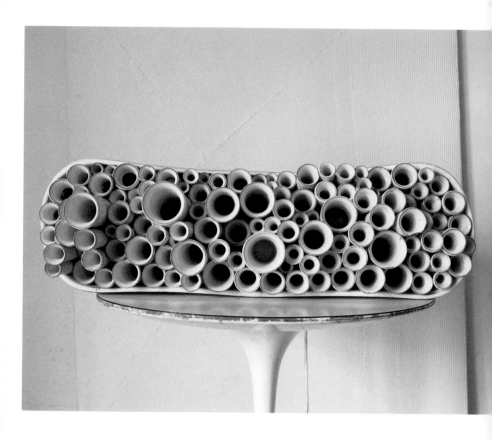

↑ This 1960s "objet d'art lamp" has found a perfect niche in the living room. • Ein anonymes Lichtobjekt aus den 1960er-Jahren macht sich sehr gut im Wohnzimmer. • Un objet-luminaire anonyme des « sixties » a trouvé sa place dans le séjour.

→ Directoire armchairs and 'toiles de Jouy' fabric have been replaced by a stylish 1950s garden chair, a Knoll coffee table and a carefully chosen collection of artwork. • Ein Gartenstuhl aus den 1950er-Jahren, ein Couchtisch von Knoll und einige ausgewählte Kunstwerke sind an die Stelle von Directoire-Sesseln und Toile-de-Jouy-Stoffen getreten. • Une chaise de jardin des années 1950, une table basse signée Knoll et quelques œuvres d'art bien choisies ont remplacé les fauteuils Directoire et les toiles de Jouy.

↑ In the bedroom, Méchiche combines a classic-looking bed draped in white linen with an acrylic-glass console topped by a 1960s lamp. • Im Schlafzimmer blieb Frédéric, trotz Plexiglastischchen und Sechzigerjahre-Lampe, dem weiß bezogenen Doppelbett treu. • Dans sa chambre à coucher, Frédéric est resté fidèle au grand lit drapé de lin blanc et a choisi pour l'accompagner une console en Altuglas et une lampe « sixties ».

→ An antique cross is juxtaposed with an acrylic-glass table and a 1960s lamp and chair, all set off in an 18th-century decor. Méchiche has proved his audacity by taking the best of each era. • Ein altes Kruzifix, ein Plexiglastischchen, eine Lampe und ein Sessel aus den 1960ern in einer Umgebung aus dem 18. Jahrhundert – Méchiche ist ein Stilmix mit dem Schönsten aus der jeweiligen Zeit gelungen. • Une croix

ancienne, une console en Altuglas, lampe et siège des années 1960 dans un décor 18ᵉ – Méchiche a réussi ce mélange en choisissant le meilleur de chaque époque.

VILLA MARIE
RAMATUELLE

It was the "Années folles", the crazy years between the First and the Second World War when the Côte d'Azur attracted painters such as Pablo Picasso and Henri Matisse and authors like Somerset Maugham, Aldous Huxley and Colette, as well as Europe's high nobility, first and foremost Edward VIII and Wallis Simpson. Its climate and its landscapes, its light and its colours made the Blue Coast a dream destination par excellence. Today the aura of this era has unfortunately disappeared in most places – anyone wishing to experience the region as the artists and bohemians of yesteryear did has to know the area well and include establishments such as the Villa Marie on the travel itinerary. Jocelyne and Jean-Louis Sibuet have designed the property as a tribute to the Côte d'Azur's finest hour. Far removed from the tourist hustle and bustle and situated in a park with palms, pines and cacti, the villa has the appearance of a luxurious private house. The mixture of Baroque armchairs and Provençal wrought-iron furniture, fat-bellied vases and delicate shells, sparkling crystal lights and classic Doric columns sounds bold, but emerges as a total work of art with as much style as charm.

Es waren die „Années folles", die verrückten Jahre zwischen dem Ersten und Zweiten Weltkrieg, als die Côte d'Azur Maler wie Pablo Picasso und Henri Matisse anzog, Schriftsteller wie Somerset Maugham, Aldous Huxley und Colette sowie Europas Hochadel, allen voran Edward VIII. und Wallis Simpson. Ihr Klima und ihre Landschaften, ihr Licht und ihre Farben machten die blaue Küste zum Traumziel par excellence. Heute ist das Flair dieser Epoche leider an den meisten Orten verflogen – wer die Region wie einst die Künstler und Bohemiens erleben möchte, muss sich gut auskennen und Adressen wie die Villa Marie auf seine Reiseroute setzen. Jocelyne und Jean-Louis Sibuet haben das Anwesen als Hommage an die schönsten Zeiten der Côte d'Azur gestaltet. Abseits vom Touristentrubel und in einem Park mit Palmen, Pinien und Kakteen gelegen, wirkt die Villa wie ein luxuriöses Privathaus. Die Mischung aus barocken Sesseln und provenzalischen Eisenmöbeln, dickbauchigen Vasen und filigranen Muscheln, funkelnden Kristallleuchtern und klassisch dorischen Säulen klingt gewagt – entpuppt sich aber als Gesamtkunstwerk mit ebenso viel Stil wie Charme.

C'était les Années folles sur la Riviera française, l'époque bénie entre la Première et la Seconde Guerre mondiale lorsque la Côte d'Azur attirait des peintres comme Pablo Picasso et Henri Matisse, des écrivains comme Somerset Maugham, Aldous Huxley et Colette ainsi que la haute noblesse européenne, Édouard VIII et Wallis Simpson ayant ouvert la marche. Son climat et ses paysages, sa lumière et ses couleurs faisaient de la Côte d'Azur une destination de rêve. Malheureusement, le charme de cette époque a disparu en de nombreux endroits. Si vous voulez voir la région comme les artistes et la bohème d'autrefois, vous devez bien connaître la côte et vous rendre à des adresses comme la Villa Marie. Jocelyne et Jean-Louis Sibuet ont aménagé cette propriété en rendant hommage à la Côte d'Azur de l'entre-deux-guerres. À l'écart des touristes, cette villa nichée dans un parc planté de palmiers, de pins et de cactus, a l'air d'une luxueuse demeure privée. Le mélange des fauteuils baroques et des meubles en fer forgé provençaux, des jarres ventrues et des coquillages filigranes, des lustres en cristal étincelants et des colonnes doriques classiques est audacieux, mais crée une œuvre d'art totale harmonieuse et séduisante.

PP. 338–339 From the terrace, the guests at Villa Marie have a Hollywood-style view of the surrounding countryside and the sea. "La Dolce Vita" is not only a Fellini film, it's also a way of life! • Von der Terrasse aus bietet sich den Gästen der Villa Marie ein Blick wie aus einem Hollywood-Film aufs Meer und die Landschaft. „La Dolce Vita" ist nicht nur ein Film von Fellini, sondern auch eine Lebenseinstellung! • De la terrasse, les hôtes de le Villa Marie ont une vue Hollywoodienne sur le paysage environnant et la mer. « La Dolce Vita » n'est pas seulement un film de Fellini mais également un art de vivre !

P. 341 You don't need much imagination to understand why the beautiful people of those crazy, Roaring Twenties visited the villa. Let's follow their example and sit down on the terrace – it's time for a reviving cocktail... • Man braucht nicht viel Fantasie, um sich vorzustellen, warum die bessere Gesellschaft der Goldenen Zwanziger die Villa besuchte. Folgen wir doch ihrem Beispiel und bestellen einen erfrischenden Cocktail auf der Terrasse ... • Il ne faut pas beaucoup d'imagination pour comprendre pourquoi le beau monde des années folles fréquentait la villa. Suivons leur exemple et asseyons-nous sur la terrasse, le temps d'un cocktail rafraîchissant...

↑ The French door of this room opens out onto a dreamy terrace where guests can eat breakfast as soon as they jump out of bed. • Die Fenstertür des Zimmers öffnet sich direkt auf die Veranda, wo die Gäste morgens ganz ungestört frühstücken können. • La porte-fenêtre d'une des chambres s'ouvre sur une terrasse de rêve qui permet aux hôtes de prendre leur petit déjeuner au saut du lit.

→ The opulent decor and Baroque furniture which furnishes this lounge at the Villa Marie would not have disappointed the Great Gatsby. • Opulentes Dekor und barocke Möbel im Salon der Villa Marie hätten nicht einmal den Geschmack für Prunk des großen Gatsby enttäuscht. • La décoration opulente et le mobilier baroque qui meuble un salon de la Villa Marie n'auraient point déplu au goût du faste du Great Gatsby.

→ A loveseat of red velvet in the Napoleon III style dominates the centre of the reception room. Its intricate shape forms a striking contrast with the yellow walls and the rest of the furniture. • Ein mit rotem Samt bezogenes „tête-à-tête" aus der Zeit Napoleons III. in der Mitte der Rezeption dominiert mit seinen geschwungenen Formen den Raum und kreiert einen spannenden Kontrast zu den gelben Wänden und dem übrigen Mobiliar. • Un « confident » de style Napoléon III recouvert de velours rouge trône au beau milieu de la pièce de réception et sa forme tarabiscotée forme un contraste saisissant avec les murs jaunes et le reste du mobilier.

PP. 346–347 The very beautiful herringbone-patterned fabric which has been chosen for the curtains also covers the headboard. The whole ensemble emanates that discreet elegance which goes hand in hand with a charming hotel. • Der schöne Stoff im Fischgrätenmuster findet sich in den Vorhängen und schmückt auch das Kopfende des Bettes. Hier zeitigt alles die diskrete Eleganz eines charmanten Hotels. • Le très beau tissu en « point de Hongrie » qui a été choisi pour les rideaux revêt aussi la tête de lit. Le tout émane l'élégance discrète qui va de pair avec un hôtel de charme.

VILLA BELLEVUE

VILLA BELLEVUE

JAN & MONIQUE DES BOUVRIE
BAIE DES CANOUBIERS, SAINT-TROPEZ

Jan des Bouvrie's renown as a designer and interior architect has spread far beyond his native Netherlands. In collaboration with his wife, Monique, a passionate advocate of audacious forms and colour, Jan has developed a signature interior style based on minimalism, pared-down design and the omnipresence of his favourite colour, white. Des Bouvrie has long been an ardent admirer of the Provence and the laidback lifestyle of the Midi and always regretted selling his villa near Saint-Tropez. So when he saw this magnificent Belle Epoque villa offering sweeping views across the Baie des Canoubiers, he bought it without a moment's hesitation. The designer admits his impulsive gesture ended up costing him dearly, for when he first laid eyes on the Villa Bellevue it was little more than a magnificent ruin. What's more, the villa's elaborate columned balcony and ochre façade were diametrically opposed to his design tastes. However, Jan managed to impose his Huguenot signature on the Bellevue, adding two new wings, a swimming pool and a spacious terrace, and painting the façade and interior white. The new-look Villa is filled with contemporary artwork and furniture designed by des Bouvrie himself.

Sein Ruf als Designer und Innenarchitekt reicht weit über die Grenzen der Niederlande hinaus. Unterstützt wird er von seiner Frau Monique, die ganz auf gewagte Farben und Formen setzt. Der schöne hugenottische Name des Bouvrie steht für Interieurs, die sich durch Klarheit und allgegenwärtiges Weiß auszeichnen. Jan liebt die Provence und schätzt den entspannten Lebensstil des Midi. Der Verkauf seines Hauses bei Saint-Tropez tat ihm später so leid, dass er keinen Augenblick zögerte, als man ihm eine große Belle-Epoque-Villa mit atemberaubendem Blick über die Bucht von Canoubiers anbot. Heute räumt des Bouvrie ein, dass ihn seine spontane Zusage viel Geld gekostet hat, denn das Haus war damals eine Ruine. Mit ihrem säulenverzierten Balkon und der ockerfarbenen Fassade entsprach die Villa zunächst nicht Jans Geschmack. Erst mit zwei weiteren Flügeln, einem Pool, einer großen Terrasse und dem durchgehend weißen Anstrich drückte Jan dem Haus seinen Stempel auf. Heute enthält die Villa eine Fülle zeitgenössischer Kunst und vom Hausherrn selbst entworfener Möbel.

Il a acquis une solide réputation de designer et architecte d'intérieur bien au-delà des frontières des Pays-Bas. Secondé par sa femme Monique qui ne jure que par les couleurs et les formes audacieuses, Jan des Bouvrie signe de son beau nom huguenot des intérieurs qui se font remarquer par leur aspect épuré et par l'omniprésence du blanc, la couleur préférée du créateur. Grand amateur de la Provence et fasciné par la vie décontractée que l'on mène dans le Midi, il a toujours regretté d'avoir vendu sa villa du côté de Saint-Tropez. Lorsqu'on lui a proposé une grande villa Belle Époque offrant une vue époustouflante sur la Baie des Canoubiers, il n'a pas hésité une seconde. Aujourd'hui, Des Bouvrie avoue que son geste impulsif lui a coûté cher. Jolie ruine, mais ruine quand même, la villa Bellevue avec son balcon orné de colonnes et sa façade ocre ne ressemblait en rien au style qu'il affectionne, mais en ajoutant deux ailes, une piscine et une grande terrasse, et en peignant la façade et l'intérieur en blanc, Jan y a apposé sa signature.

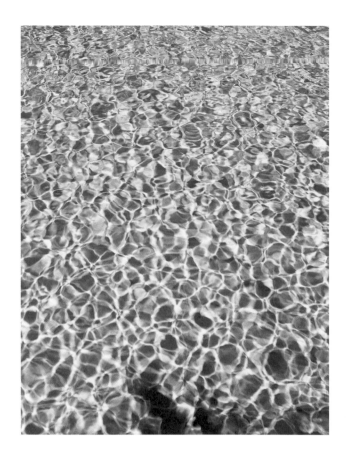

PP. 348–349 Des Bouvrie built his swimming pool against the stunning backdrop of the Baie des Canoubiers. Set between luxuriant palm trees, the pool becomes a stage and the terrace a balcony overlooking the natural theatre decor. • Des Bouvrie baute seinen Pool mit Blick auf die atemberaubende Baie des Canoubiers. Eingefasst von prachtvollen Palmen wird das Becken zur Bühne, die Terrasse zur Loge und das Ganze erscheint wie eine Theaterkulisse • Des Bouvrie a placé sa piscine face à la splendide Baie des Canoubiers. Limitée par des palmiers luxuriants, la piscine devient un podium, la terrasse

un balcon et l'ensemble un décor de théâtre.

P. 351 With its dazzling white walls and its columned veranda, Bellevue looks like a colonial mansion in the Caribbean. • Mit seinem blendenden Weiß und der Säulenveranda erinnert die Villa Bellevue an den karibischen Kolonialstil. • Avec sa blancheur éclatante et sa véranda à colonnes, Bellevue arbore un faux air de maison coloniale style Caraïbes.

← Jan has constructed a small terrace behind the house, enclosing the private

space with four low walls. • Hinter dem Haus ließ Jan eine kleine Terrasse anlegen und mit vier halbhohen Mauern einfassen. • Derrière la maison, Jan a construit une petite terrasse en entourant l'espace restreint de quatre murs bas.

↑ The reflection cast by the sun in the swimming pool has the allure of a contemporary artwork. • Das vom Schwimmbecken reflektierte Sonnenlicht gerät zu einem natürlichen modernen Kunstwerk. • Les reflets du soleil dans la piscine créent un tableau contemporain composé par la nature.

PP. 354–355 While Jan is the high priest of black-and-white minimalism, Monique's tastes run to bold splashes of colour such as bright orange floor cushions and a tangerine-coloured rug. • Während Jan der Hohepriester eines minimalistischen schwarz-weißen Stils ist, liebt Monique die Pracht der Farben. Ihrer Fantasie entstammen die Sitzkissen und der orangefarbene Teppich. • Si Jan est le grand prêtre du noir et blanc, Monique est une magicienne de la couleur. C'est à elle que l'on doit les grands coussins et le tapis orange.

↑ Monique, a talented stylist, has added innovative design touches to the house worthy of the best interiors magazine. • Monique ist Gestalterin mit Leib und Seele. Ihr eigenes Heim richtete sie wie für eines der großen Innenarchitekturmagazine ein. • Styliste de grand talent, Monique gère son intérieur comme s'il devait être reproduit dans un grand magazine de décoration.

→ The interior also bears the mark of the designer known as the "white tornado". • Auch das Interieur trägt die

Handschrift des Hausherrn, der hier seinem Spitznamen „weißer Wirbelwind" gerecht wird. • L'intérieur aussi porte la signature de celui qu'on a surnommé « la tornade blanche ».

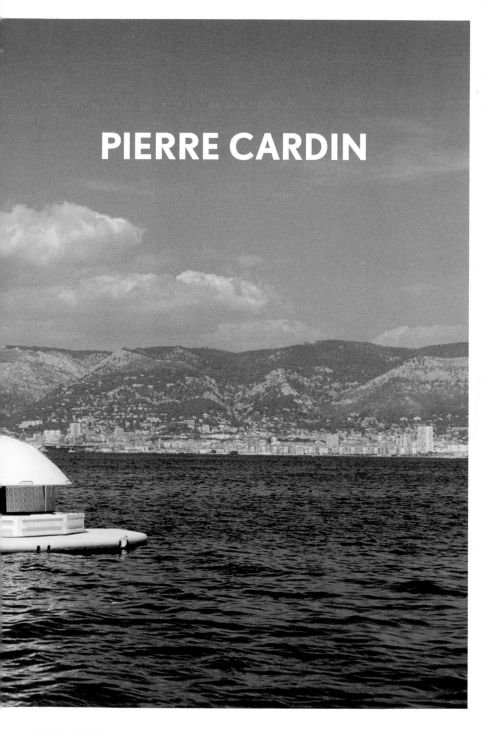

PIERRE CARDIN

PIERRE CARDIN
SAINT-TROPEZ

The name of Pierre Cardin's floating habitat – "Anthénéa" – is derived from the Greek word for blossom. Its design was inspired by the final scene of The Spy Who Loved Me, in which James Bond escapes with his lover in a sea capsule. The brainwave of French architect Jean-Michel Ducancelle, it is made from fibreglass and has a glass bottom, which allows you to admire marine life close-up. "It's very relaxing," says Ducancelle. "You feel like you're actually floating in the water." It's also more stable than a boat. "It can resist a cyclone," he adds. Cardin has fitted his capsule out in the pure 1970s style, with black-and-white fabrics. A larger version has a built-in jacuzzi, as well as a Bang & Olufsen hi-fi system and wireless Internet hook-ups. "There are lots of gadgets," states Ducancelle. "That way, you can really play at being James Bond."

Der Name von Pierre Cardins schwimmendem Wohnobjekt – „Anthénéa" – ist von dem griechischen Wort für „Blüte" abgeleitet. Und dessen Entwurf ist von der letzten Szene des Films „Der Spion, der mich liebte" inspiriert, in der sich James Bond samt Gespielin in einer wasserdichten Kapsel an Land rettet. Die Idee zu der Seekapsel stammt von dem französischen Architekten Jean-Michel Ducancelle. Sie besteht aus Fiberglas und hat einen Glasboden, durch den man das Leben unter Wasser aus nächster Nähe beobachten kann. „Das ist ebenso entspannend", sagt Ducancelle, „als wäre man selbst im Wasser." Die Kapsel ist stabiler als ein Schiff. „Sie kann einem Zyklon trotzen", fügt er hinzu. Cardin hat sie im Stil der 1970er-Jahre ganz in kontrastierendem Schwarz-Weiß eingerichtet. Die größere Variante hat einen eingebauten Whirlpool sowie eine Hi-Fi-Anlage von Bang & Olufsen und einen drahtlosen Internet-Anschluss. „Mit diesem technischen Equipment", meint Ducancelle, „kann man selbst James Bond spielen."

Le cocon flottant de Pierre Cardin, Anthénéa, doit son nom au mot grec pour « éclosion ». Son design a été inspiré par la scène finale de « L'Espion qui m'aimait », où James Bond s'échappait avec la belle à bord d'une capsule amphibie. Son concepteur, l'architecte Jean-Michel Ducancelle, l'a réalisé en fibre de verre et équipé d'un fond transparent pour admirer la faune marine. « C'est très relaxant. On a la sensation de flotter sur l'eau », affirme-t-il. Il est également plus stable qu'un bateau et « peut résister à un cyclone ». Cardin l'a décoré dans le pur style des années 70, avec des tissus graphiques noirs et blancs. Il existe une version plus grande avec jacuzzi, un système hi-fi Bang & Olufsen et une connexion Internet sans fil. « Il y a plein de gadgets pour se mettre à la place de James Bond », confie Ducancelle.

PP. 364–365 An anchor-like sculpture stands on a maple-veneer table, which can be lowered into the floor. • Eine Skulptur, die an einen Anker erinnert, steht auf einem im Boden versenkbaren Tisch mit Ahornfurnier. • Une sculpture en forme d'ancre sur une table plaquée en érable qui peut descendre au ras du sol.

← ↑ Cardin opted to use black-and-white op-art fabrics throughout the interior. • Cardin entschied sich bei der gesamten Inneneinrichtung für Stoffe in kontrastierendem Schwarz-Weiß. • Pour l'intérieur, Cardin a opté pour des tissus imprimés de motifs noirs et blancs créant des illusions d'optique.

PASTIS HÔTEL ST TROPEZ

PASTIS HÔTEL ST TROPEZ

The longing for sun, sea air and summer holidays attracted first the aristocracy and high society from grey Great Britain southwards – and later the painters and authors, the stars and the starlets were to follow. Among the most famous of the recent British coast-dwellers was the the author Peter Mayle, who devoted several books to the convergence of English eccentricity and French finesse. One of them bears the title "Hotel Pastis" – and John and Pauline Larkin's guest house owes its name to this work. The couple (how could it be otherwise!) came from London to Saint-Tropez, and the former graphic designer and his wife have restored a Provençal villa in masterly fashion and given it a touch of the London lifestyle: they mix beds in the style of the French country house, Chinese wardrobes and design classics such as those by Mies van der Rohe, adding opulent mirrors, mighty copper bathtubs and modern art prints by David Hockney and Roy Lichtenstein. All rooms offer a patio, a balcony or a terrace; the wonderful veranda outside room 4 measures nearly 200 square feet and looks out over the pool to the sea.

Die Sehnsucht nach Sonne, Seeluft und Sommerfrische ließ zunächst Adel und High Society aus dem grauen Großbritannien gen Süden ziehen – später folgten die Maler und Schriftsteller, Stars und Sternchen. Zu den berühmtesten britischen Küstenbewohnern zählte lange Peter Mayle, der dem Zusammentreffen englischer Exzentrik und französischer Finesse mehrere Bücher gewidmet hat. Eines davon trägt den Titel „Hotel Pastis" – ihm verdankt das charmante Gästehaus von John und Pauline Larkin seinen Namen. Die Larkins kamen (wie könnte es anders sein!) aus London nach Saint-Tropez. Der ehemalige Grafikdesigner und seine Frau haben eine provenzalische Villa restauriert und ihr eine Spur Londoner Lifestyle verliehen: Sie mischen Betten im französischen Landhausstil, chinesische Schränke sowie Designklassiker etwa von Mies van der Rohe mit opulenten Spiegeln, mächtigen Kupferwannen und Kunstdrucken von David Hockney und Roy Lichtenstein. Alle Räume bieten einen Patio, einen Balkon oder eine Terrasse; die wunderbare Veranda vor Zimmer 4 misst sogar 18 Quadratmeter und blickt auf den Pool und bis zum Meer.

Le désir de soleil, d'air marin et de vacances a tout d'abord incité les nobles et la High Society à quitter la Grande-Bretagne brumeuse pour le Midi, plus tard les peintres et écrivains, stars et starlettes les ont rejoints. L'auteur Peter Mayle etait un des plus célèbres résidents britanniques de la Côte, où il avait commencé à écrire une série de livres sur la rencontre entre l'excentricité britannique et le raffinement français. « Hôtel Pastis », un de ses best-sellers, a inspiré deux Londoniens, John et Pauline Larkin, venus s'installer (bien évidemment!) à Saint-Tropez et qui ont donné le nom de ce roman à leur charmant hôtel. L'ancien graphiste et sa femme ont admirablement restauré cette villa provençale et lui ont conféré une touche de Lifestyle londonien. Ils combinent les lits de campagne, les armoires chinoises ainsi que des classiques du design comme ceux de Mies van der Rohe, ajoutant des miroirs opulents, des baignoires en cuivre imposantes et des reproductions modernes de David Hockney et Roy Lichtenstein. Toutes les pièces disposent d'un patio, d'un balcon ou d'une terrasse, la splendide véranda de la chambre 4 mesure même 18 mètres carrés et donne sur la piscine et sur la mer.

PP. 368–369 Looking at this patio adorned with palm trees and a pool, one immediately recognises the atmosphere running through the books of the late Peter Mayle. A Year in Provence would not be sufficient to fully benefit from the delights of the Pastis Hôtel! • Beim Blick auf diesen Innenhof mit Pool und Palmen hat man sofort die Bücher von Peter Mayle vor Augen. Doch ein Jahr in der Provence genügte wohl kaum, um alle Vorzüge des Pastis Hotel zu genießen! • En observant ce patio agrémenté de palmiers et d'une piscine, on reconnaît immédiatement l'ambiance qui règne

dans les livres du regretté Peter Mayle. Une année en Provence ne suffirait pas pour profiter pleinement des délices du Pastis Hôtel !

P. 371 Can you get more French than this breakfast on the terrace? The benevolent sun will do the rest... • Was könnte noch französischer sein als dieses Frühstück auf der Terrasse? Und über allem strahlt die Sonne ... • Plus français que ce petit dej' sur la terrasse n'existe pas. Le soleil bienfaisant s'occupe du reste.

PP. 372–373 The stools are contemporary, but the atmosphere is one hundred percent southern France. We could almost expect to see Marius and Olive with their elbows resting on the zinc counter, sipping a pastis. • Die Hocker mögen von heute sein, aber der Rest ist hundertprozentig Mittelmeer. Hier könnten auch die Filmhelden Marius und Olive einen Pastis schlürfen. • Les tabourets sont contemporains mais l'ambiance dans le bar est cent pour cent méridional. On s'y attend de voir Marius et Olive qui sirotent un pastis accoudés au zinc.

← The four-poster bed covered in white echoes the immaculate whiteness of the walls. In this simple yet comfortable room the decor gives off a pleasant coolness. • Ein Himmelbett ganz in Weiß vor makellos weißen Wänden. Dieses einfach gehaltene, aber komfortable Zimmer verströmt angenehme Kühle. • Le lit à colonnes habillé de blanc fait écho à la blancheur immaculée des murs et dans cette chambre simple et confortable la décoration émane une fraîcheur agréable.

↓ The rococo bed in the Belle Époque style and the large mirror with the golden frame give this room an untypical and very glamorous atmosphere. • Das Bett aus der Belle Epoque lässt die Formen des Rokoko wieder aufleben. Zusammen mit dem großen Spiegel im Goldrahmen verleiht es diesem Zimmer eine ungewohnt glamouröse Atmosphäre. • Le lit « rococo » style Belle Epoque et le grand miroir au cadre doré donnent à cette chambre une ambiance atypique et très « glamour ».

HÔTEL DU CAP-EDEN-ROC
CAP D'ANTIBES

There are hotels that seem more than the sum of their parts, and then there's the Cap-Eden-Roc, where everything seems straight out of a dream. Cream-coloured residence by the sea. Perfectly manicured grounds with a path (a catwalk?) to the coast. Seafront pool carved into the rock, by which guests sunbathe in almost obligatory Eres bikinis. Suites with Louis XVI–style interiors. Not forgetting the restaurant with yacht-deck-like terrace and the stunning piano bar. No wonder Leonardo DiCaprio, Cate Blanchett, and Sean Connery all hole up at this Cap d'Antibes hideaway during the Cannes Film Festival. Behind the scenes, everything here runs like clockwork: the Cap-Eden-Roc is a celebration of the hotelier's art and of old-school Riviera luxury. Until a few years ago, it had no in-room TVs, provided hai- dryers only on request, and didn't take credit cards. This is a place where other things matter more: absolute discretion, for example, or the private-club atmosphere.

Es gibt Hotels, die mehr sind als die Summe ihrer Annehmlichkeiten, und noch darüber schwebt das Cap-Eden-Roc. Ein cremefarbener Palast am Meer, ein makellos manikürter Park, durch den ein Weg, nein: Laufsteg zur Küste mit einem Felsenpool führt, an dessen Rand man gefälligst im Eres-Bikini sonnenbadet. Nicht zu vergessen Suiten im Louis-XVI-Stil, ein Restaurant mit einem veritablen Jachtdeck von Terrasse und eine hinreißende Pianobar. Kein Wunder, dass während des Filmfestivals in Cannes hier Leonardo DiCaprio, Cate Blanchett und Sean Connery verweilen. Wie in den Filmstudios läuft hinter den Kulissen eine wahre Präzisionsmaschine: Das Haus am Cap d'Antibes zelebriert die Hotellerie alter Schule, als Sehnsuchtsort klassischer Riviera-Sommerfrische. Bis vor wenigen Jahren kamen die Zimmer ohne Fernseher aus, Haartrockner wurden nur auf Wunsch gebracht und Kreditkarten nicht akzeptiert. In diesen Hallen setzt man eben auf andere Werte: zum Beispiel auf formvollendete Diskretion und Club-Gefühl.

Certains hôtels offrent plus encore que ce qu'ils annoncent. Le Cap-Eden-Roc va même au-delà. Un palais couleur crème, un parc tiré à quatre épingles traversé par un chemin, ou plutôt un « tapis rouge » bis menant à une piscine creusée dans la roche au-dessus de la mer et sur les bords de laquelle il est de bon ton de prendre un bain de soleil en bikini Eres. Sans oublier les suites de style Louis XVI, un restaurant avec un pont de yacht en guise de terrasse et un merveilleux piano-bar. Pas étonnant que Leonardo DiCaprio, Cate Blanchett et Sean Connery s'y attardent pendant le Festival de Cannes. Comme dans les studios de cinéma, c'est une machine de précision qui fonctionne dans les coulisses : ce lieu mythique de la villégiature classique sur la Côte d'Azur perpétue la tradition hôtelière à l'ancienne. Il y a quelques années encore, les chambres n'avaient pas de téléviseur, le sèche-cheveux était apporté sur demande et les cartes bancaires n'étaient pas acceptées. Ici, c'est la discrétion absolue et l'ambiance club qui priment.

PP. 376–377 No, this isn't a mirage – it's the Hôtel du Cap-Eden Roc, the legendary palace idyllically located on the rocks of Cap d'Antibes. During the Cannes Film Festival, the hotel is one of the preferred addresses of the big stars. • Keine Sinnestäuschung, sondern der legendäre Palast des Hotels Cap-Eden-Roc, idyllisch auf den Felsen des Cap d'Antibes gelegen, wohin sich während der Filmfestspiele von Cannes bevorzugt die Stars zurückziehen. • Non, ceci n'est pas un mirage mais l'Hôtel du Cap-Eden Roc , le palace mythique qui domine les rochers du Cap d'Antibes. Pendant le festival de Cannes, l'hôtel est une des adresses préférées des plus grandes stars du cinéma.

P. 379 We can't imagine a better place for breakfast: this is ideal. The terrace, with its classical balustrade and the view

of the park and the sea, seems to have come straight out of a novel by Somerset Maugham. • Man könnte sich keinen schöneren Ort fürs Frühstück vorstellen: diese Terrasse, mit ihrer klassischen Balustrade und dem Blick auf Park und Meer ist ideal dafür. Sie scheint einem Roman von Somerset Maugham entsprungen. • On ne peut pas s'imaginer un endroit plus idéal pour prendre le petit déjeuner. La terrasse avec sa balustrade classique et sa vue sur le parc et la mer, semble sortir tout droit d'une nouvelle signée Somerset Maugham.

← The founder of "Le Figaro" newspaper, Hippolyte de Villemessant, constructed the hotel in 1870, at the end of the reign of Napoleon III. It is still one of the most sumptuous palaces along the coast. • Der Gründer der Tageszeitung „Le Figaro", Hippolyte de Villemessant,

baute das Haus im Jahr 1870, am Ende der Herrschaft Napoleons III. Noch heute ist der Palast einer der prächtigsten entlang der Küste. • Construit en 1870 par Hippolyte de Villemessant, le créateur du journal « Le Figaro », le bâtiment qui date de la fin du règne de Napoléon III est un des palaces les plus somptueux de la côte.

↑ Looking down at the pool carved out of the rock and its adjoining terrace, you can believe that you're on the bridge of a luxurious cruise liner. • Man glaubt sich auf einem Luxuscruiser, wenn man die Terrasse hinunterschaut auf den Pool, der aus dem Felsen herausgearbeitet wurde. • En regardant la piscine creusée dans la roche et sa terrasse attenante on a l'impression de voir le pont d'un luxueux bateau de croisière.

PP. 382–383 A style to die for! And the bar, with its neoclassical decor and armchairs in yellow and white tones, is a cocktail venue par excellence. • So chic! Und die Bar im neoklassischen Dekor mit Sesseln in Gelb und Weiß ist der perfekte Ort, um einen Cocktail zu trinken. • Plus chic on meurt ! Et le bar avec son décor néo-classique et ses fauteuils houssés dans les tons jaune et blanc est l'endroit par excellence pour boire un cocktail.

↑ The bar decor has a perfect symmetry, and white panelling frames the wall paintings that depict landscapes of southern France. • In der Bar ist die Einrichtung perfekt symmetrisch, und weiße Wandvertäfelungen rahmen die Landschaftsmalereien ein. • Dans le bar le décor est d'une symétrie parfaite et les lambris blancs s'ornent de peintures murales qui représentent des paysages du midi de la France.

→ The covered terrace is being prepared for dinner, and pretty multi-coloured bouquets will soon be in place on the tables. • Die überdachte Terrasse wird für das Abendessen vorbereitet, und die hübschen Blumenbouquets werden bald die Tische farbig auffrischen. • On prépare la terrasse couverte pour le dîner et de jolis bouquets multicolores vont bientôt retrouver leur place sur les tables.

↑ All the classics you could wish for: the decoration of the hotel suites was inspired by the timeless elegance of certain Parisian hotels. · Die Einrichtung in den Suiten des Hotels wurde inspiriert von der zeitlosen Eleganz Pariser Stadtpalais. · Classiques à souhait, les suites de l'hôtel ont été décoré en s'inspirant de l'élégance intemporelle des hôtels particuliers Parisiens.

→ The guests who come to Eden-Roc appreciate the charm of a distant era and the no-frills decor that is at the other end of the scale from a flashy, bling style. · Die Gäste des Hotels schätzen sowohl den Charme einer vergangenen Zeit als auch die schnörkellose Dekoration, die nicht nach Aufmerksamkeit heischt. · Les clients qui viennent loger à l'Eden-Roc y apprécient le charme d'une époque lointaine et la décoration sans fioritures qui se tient loin du « m'as-tu vu ».

↑ In this suite, so elegantly furnished,
Marlene Dietrich or the Duchess of
Windsor would feel completely at home.
We understand why Hôtel du Cap is
an oasis for celebrities from all over the
world... • In dieser eleganten Suite
braucht man nicht viel Fantasie, um sich
die Anwesenheit von Marlene Dietrich
oder der Herzogin von Windsor auszu-
malen, und man versteht sofort, warum
die Crème de la Crème im Hotel du
Cap Ruhe sucht ... • Dans cette suite au
décor raffiné on ne doit faire aucun
effort pour s'imaginer la présence de
Marlène Dietrich ou la Duchesse de
Windsor et on comprend pourquoi les
grands de ce monde viennent se refu-
gier à l'Hôtel du Cap...

CAP ESTEL

CAP ESTEL
ÈZE-BORD-DE-MER

This French Riviera hotel is blessed (there's no other word for it) with a spectacular location. Situated on a peninsula between Nice and Monte Carlo, its four villas boast stunning views of the Mediterranean, while also offering high levels of privacy. That, no doubt, is why the Cap Estel has long been a popular hideaway among more discerning members of the international jet set. The hotel was built in 1900 by Frank Harris, an Irish journalist and friend of Oscar Wilde. He was succeeded as owner by Baron Stroganoff, who, in turn, was followed by shipping dynasty scion and surrealist poet Andreas Embiricos. The ocean views are not the only natural attraction, however – the grounds to the rear are full of rare trees. The suites' interiors, meanwhile, offer the kind of grand Mediterranean style that never fails to lift the spirits after a day in the sun. Alternatively, guests can cool off in the seafront saltwater infinity pool – the perfect place to lie back and think of love, life, and money.

Man kann es nicht anders nennen: Das Cap Estel liegt in gebenedeiter Lage. Auf einer Halbinsel zwischen Nizza und Monte Carlo eröffnen seine vier Villen den Bewohnern der Suiten sagenhafte Aussichten aufs Mittelmeer und bieten zugleich viel Privatsphäre. Wohl deshalb ist das Kap schon lange Anlaufstelle für Mitglieder des kultivierten Jetsets. Bauherr im Jahre 1900 war Frank Harris, ein irischer Journalist und Freund Oscar Wildes, ihm folgten ein Baron Stroganoff sowie der griechische Reederei-Erbe und surrealistische Dichter Andreas Embiricos. Hier ist nicht nur der Meerblick hinreißend, sondern auch die Rückseite mit einem Park voll ausgesucht seltener Bäume. Die Zimmer sind in jener mediterranen Noblesse eingerichtet, die am Ende eines Tags an der Sonne so aufmunternd wirkt. Natürlich kann man auch in den Infinity-Salzwasserpool steigen, der mit seiner grandios exponierten Lage dazu einlädt, sich schwerelos treiben zu lassen und über das Leben, die Liebe und das Geld nachzudenken, irgendwo zwischen Nizza und Monte Carlo.

Le Cap Estel jouit indéniablement d'une situation géographique privilégiée. Trônant sur une presqu'île entre Nice et Monte-Carlo, ses quatre villas offrent une vue sublime sur la mer Méditerranée et beaucoup d'intimité. C'est pourquoi le Cap Estel accueille depuis longtemps les représentants de la jet-set distinguée. Construit en 1900 par Frank Harris, journaliste irlandais et ami d'Oscar Wilde, le domaine a plus tard appartenu au baron Stroganoff puis à Andréas Embiríkos, poète surréaliste et héritier d'une dynastie d'armateurs grecs. Si côté mer, la vue est magique, elle est tout aussi somptueuse côté jardin, avec le parc planté d'essences rares. Les chambres sont aménagées avec raffinement dans cet esprit méditerranéen chaleureux qui requinque après une journée au soleil. On peut aussi profiter bien sûr de la piscine d'eau de mer à débordement qui invite à se laisser bercer par l'apesanteur pour méditer sur la vie, l'amour et l'argent – quelque part entre Nice et Monte-Carlo.

PP. 390–391 The four villas perching at the edge of the almost private island of Cap Estel offer their guests an unforgettable view of the blue waters of the Mediterranean. • Die vier Villas auf der Anhöhe der privaten Halbinsel Cap Estel bieten ihren Gästen einen einzigartigen Ausblick auf das blau schimmernde Mittelmeer. • Les quatre villas qui se perchent sur les hauteurs de la presqu'île privée du Cap Estel offrent à leurs hôtes une vue inoubliable sur les eaux bleues de la Méditerranée.

P. 393 The private beach adjoining the hotel is a unique bathing indulgence! • Der Privatstrand beim Hotel verspricht ein einzigartiges Badevergnügen! • La plage privée jouxtant l'hôtel procure un plaisir balnéaire unique.

← The private patios are decorated with baroque stone urns and potted plants. These rattan loungers are so tempting, and perfect for a lazy afternoon ... • Die einzelnen Innenhöfe wurden mit barocken Steinurnen und Pflanzen dekoriert. Die Lounge-Sessel aus Rattan sind sehr einladend und perfekt geeignet für's Faulenzen ... • Les patios privés on été décoré avec des vasques en pierre baroques et des plantes en pot. Des chaises longues en rotin tressé invitent à la paresse...

↓ The majestic front gates in period style are cast in wrought iron and are a match for the proud appearance of an old château entrance. • Das grandiose historische Eingangstor aus Schmiedeeisen würde auch einem Schloss zur Ehre gereichen. • La majestueuse grille d'entrée d'époque à été réalisée en fer forgé et elle égale la fière allure d'une ancienne entrée de château.

PP. 396–397 On the patio side of the hotel, a private garden has been blessed with a lawn. Palm crowns extend their protective shadow over the façade. • Zum Innenhof liegt ein privater Garten mit Rasenfläche. Die Kronen der Palmen werfen einen schützenden Schatten auf die Fassade. • Côté patio, un jardin privatif a été doté d'un carré de gazon. Les couronnes des palmiers projettent une ombre protectrice sur la façade.

↑ At Cap Estel the grand reception area (one deliberately avoids the term "lobby"), with its built-in cabinet-bookcases, fireplace, 18th-century tapestry, comfortable armchairs and grand piano, attest to an illustrious past. • Die glanzvolle Geschichte von Cap Estel spiegelt sich im Empfangszimmer (hier wird nicht von „Lobby" gesprochen), mit seiner Bibliothek, dem Kamin, Teppichen des 18. Jahrhunderts, komfortablen Sesseln und dem prächtigen Flügel. • Au Cap Estel le grand salon de réception (on évite exprès le nom « lobby ») avec ses armoire-bibliothèque encastrées, sa cheminée, sa tapisserie dix-huitième, ses fauteuils confortables et son piano à queue, témoigne d'un passé prestigieux.

→ The style of the bar takes its inspiration from the famous grand hotel bars of the 1930s. The warm tone of the mahogany marries perfectly with the light-coloured stools and the white Louis XVI-style armchairs. • Die Bar ist dekoriert im Chic der berühmten Hotelbars der Dreißigerjahre. Die Wärme des Mahagoni-Holzes passt gut zu den hellen Farben der Hocker und den weißen Sesseln im Stil Louis XVI. • La décoration du bar puise son inspiration dans les célèbres bars des grands hôtels des années 30. Le ton chaud de l'acajou se marie parfaitement aux tabourets clairs et aux fauteuils de style Louis XVI revêtus de blanc.

↑ As is customary in grand hotels, discretion is the order of the day. The presence of a luxury that has no hint of ostentation is evident in the choice of classic furniture and a mainly pastel colour scheme. • Absolute Diskretion ist in einem solchen Grand Hotel geboten. Luxus wird hier nicht zur Schau gestellt, das zeigt sich auch in der Auswahl der klassischen Möbel und der pastellfarbenen Palette. • Comme il est coutume dans les grands hôtels, le ton est à la discrétion. La présence d'un luxe qui n'a rien d'ostentatoire se manifeste dans le choix d'un mobilier classique et d'une palette de couleurs à dominante pastel.

→ Under the large, Art Deco chandelier, weighed down by dense rows of crystal beads, we can almost make out the enigmatic silhouette of one of the most famous guests of this hotel, the divine Greta Garbo, who was always looking for anonymity and solitude... • Unter dem schweren Art-Deco-Lüster mit seinen dicken Perlenschnüren meint man die schattenhafte Silhouette des berühmtesten Gastes dieses Hotels auszumachen – Greta Garbo, auf der Suche nach Anonymität und Abgeschiedenheit. • Sous le grand lustre art-déco chargé d'épaisses rangées de perles en cristal, on devine la silhouette énigmatique d'une des hôtes les plus célèbres

de l'hôtel : la divine Greta Garbo, toujours à la recherche d'anonymat et de solitude...

PP. 402–403 There is nothing more luxurious than a sumptuous hotel suite where the French windows open out onto a balcony with a view of the sea and the tops of the palm trees! • Es gibt nichts Besseres als eine prächtige Hotelsuite, deren Fenstertüren sich auf einen Balkon mit Blick auf Meer und Palmen öffnen. • Il n'existe pas de plus grand luxe qu'une suite d'hôtel somptueuse dont les porte-fenêtres sont ouvertes sur un balcon avec vue sur la mer et sur les sommets des palmiers !

← A classical balustrade, a tiled floor of tessellated white octagons and black square, and assorted outdoor furniture make this terrace the epitome of elegance. • Die Terrasse wirkt äußerst elegant durch ihre klassische Balustrade, den schwarz-weiß gemusterten Steinboden und die sorgsam ausgewählten Möbel. • Une balustrade classique, un sol en carrelage blanc incrusté de cabochons noirs et un mobilier de jardin assorti font de cette terrasse le comble de l'élégance.

↑ A suite further embellished by a mezzanine floor is decorated in blue and white tones and the result is extremely restful. • Diese Suite mit Mezzanin ist ganz in Blau und Weiß gehalten. Eine Wohltat für die Augen. • Une suite agrémentée d'une mezzanine a été décorée dans des tonalités bleues et blanches et le résultat est reposant pour les yeux.

PP. 406–407 Nothing matches the privilege of settling down on one of the comfortable terraces of this hotel to contemplate the wonderful panorama. A glass of well-chilled champagne will complement this moment of happiness! • Ein unvergleichliches Privileg, sich auf einer der Terrassen des Hotels zu entspannen und den fabelhaften Ausblick zu genießen. Ein Glas gut gekühlten Champagners vervollständigt dann das Glück! • Rien n'égale le privilège de s'installer confortablement sur une des terrasses de l'hôtel et de contempler le magnifique panorama. Un verre de champagne bien frappé complètera ce moment de bonheur.

MONTE-CARLO
BEACH

MONTE-CARLO BEACH
ROQUEBRUNE-CAP-MARTIN

In 1929, modernism arrived with a bang on the Côte d'Azur, courtesy of a luxury beach hotel that suddenly made the stuccoed grand hotels of old look overdressed. Built by celebrated architect Roger Séassal for the Société des Bains de Mer, it had the curves of a Bugatti, the sleek lines of a garçonne haircut, and an Olympic pool with diving tower – a facility that, just as at the new resorts then being built in the United States, was as much about flirting over cocktails as about sporting endeavour. Eight decades later, Parisian interior designer India Mahdavi completed a redesign of this Art Deco gem that draws on the Côte's avant-garde past – on Henri Matisse, Jean Cocteau, Eileen Gray, and even gossip queen Elsa Maxwell, who once organised the hotel's opening ball. On the subject of parties, the waterfront Sea Lounge ensures the hotel still features prominently on Monaco's social circuit. Some things never change – thankfully!

1929 zog die Moderne an der Côte d'Azur ein, und zwar mit einem echten Knaller. Im Auftrag der Société des Bains de Mer hatte der renommierte Architekt Roger Séassal ein Luxushotel an die Küste gestellt, das die Grandhotels mit ihren Stuckgirlanden auf einmal tantig wirken ließ: kurvig wie ein Bugatti, schnittig wie eine Garçonne-Frisur und mit Wettkampfpool samt Sprungturm ganz dem Sport und dem Flirten bei Cocktails gewidmet, genau wie die gleichzeitig entstehenden Resorts in den USA. Zeitsprung in die 2000er. Die Pariser Interior-Designerin India Mahdavi wird mit der Neugestaltung des Art-déco-Juwels betraut und ruft als Inspiration prompt die Geister der Côte-Avantgarde auf – von Henri Matisse, Jean Cocteau und Eileen Gray bis zur Klatschdiva Elsa Maxwell, die einst den Eröffnungsball organisierte. Apropos: Dank der Sea Lounge direkt am Meer gehört das Hotel immer noch zu Monacos besten Partyplätzen. Manche Dinge ändern sich eben nie. Zum Glück!

En 1929, l'apparition de l'architecture moderne sur la Côte d'Azur fit l'effet d'une bombe. Le célèbre architecte Roger Séassal avait été chargé par la Société des Bains de Mer de réaliser un hôtel de luxe, à côté duquel les grands hôtels croulant sous le stuc feraient soudain mauvais genre. Arborant les courbes d'une Bugatti, ce palace doté d'une piscine de compétition et d'un plongeoir devait être voué au sport et au flirt autour de cocktails, exactement comme les grands hôtels américains de la même époque. Plus tard, dans les années 2000, l'architecte d'intérieur parisienne India Mahdavi, qui se voit confier le réaménagement de ce bijou Art déco, s'inspire de l'avant-garde de la Côte d'Azur – de Henri Matisse à Elsa Maxwell, qui organisa autrefois le bal d'ouverture, en passant par Jean Cocteau et Eileen Gray. Grâce au Sea Lounge donnant sur la mer, cet hôtel compte toujours parmi les hauts lieux des fêtes monégasques. Heureusement, il est des choses qui ne changent pas.

PP. 408–409 The architecture of Monte-Carlo Beach owes much to luxury ocean liner style and just as much to the curvy forms of early 20th-century sports cars. • Die Architektur des Monte-Carlo Beach ist einerseits vom Stil der großen Luxusdampfer beeinflusst, genauso aber auch von den Kurven der Sportwagen vom Beginn des letzten Jahrhunderts. • L'architecture du Monte-Carlo Beach doit beaucoup au style des paquebots de luxe et autant aux formes curvilignes des voitures de sport du début du 20ᵉ siècle.

P. 411 On the terrace, the parasols and the cushions have marine blue piping for a striking visual effect. • Auf der Terrasse fallen die marineblauen Borten der Sonnenschirme und Kissen sofort auf. • Sur la terrasse les parasols et les coussins des sièges ont été bordés d'un passepoil bleu marine. L'effet graphique est saisissant.

PP. 412–413 The strict alignment of the palm trees, parasols and deck chairs at the edge of the pool is a great success. • Die strenge Anordnung der Palmen, Sonnenschirme und Liegen wirkt einfach großartig. • L'alignement rigoureux des palmiers, des parasols et des transats qui bordent la piscine est une grande réussite.

← In this rotunda-shaped lounge, the decor is based on a subtle play of circles and curved lines. • Diese runde Lounge bestimmt ein subtiles Spiel von Kreisen und Bogenlinien . • Dans ce salon en forme de rotonde, la décoration est dominée par un jeu subtil de cercles et de lignes incurvées.

↑ Here India Mahdavi has succeeded in creating a strong visual tension between the horizontal and vertical lines in her decor • In diesem Zimmer hat India Mahdavi ein Dekor geschaffen, das von einer Spannung zwischen der horizontalen und vertikalen Linienführung dominiert wird. • Dans cette chambre, India Mahdavi a réussi à créer un décor qui se distingue par une forte tension visuelle entre les lignes horizontales et verticales.

P. 416 For the fitted furniture, the designer was inspired by the benches built into "Riva" motorboats. A table from her "Bishop" line echoes the ocean-liner porthole in the wall above. • Die Designerin ließ sich bei der Einrichtung des Hotels von den berühmten Motorbooten der Serie „Riva" und deren eingelassenen Bänken inspirieren. Hier ein Zusammenspiel der Formen zwischen einem Tisch aus der Serie „Bishop" und der Luke im Stil der großen Ozeandampfer. • En ce qui concerne le mobilier fixe de l'hôtel, la designer s'est inspirée des banquettes encastrées

dans les bateaux à moteur du type « Riva ». Une table de sa ligne « Bishop » fait écho au hublot style paquebot.

P. 417 The restaurant layout is the perfect example of the Monte-Carlo Beach style created here by Mahdavi. Her colour scheme is based on grey and blue. • Die Gestaltung dieses Restaurants ist ein ideales Beispiel für India Mahdavis Monte-Carlo-Beach-Stil, mit einer klaren Palette von Blau- und Grautönen. • L'aménagement du restaurant est l'exemple par excellence du style « Monte Carlo Beach » créé

par Mahdavi. Son choix des couleurs est basé sur le gris et le bleu.

↑ In the corridors, the porthole-style windows are cut out of thick walls. They offer a stunning view of the Bay of Monaco. • In den Fluren ermöglichen die Bullaugen-Fenster einen traumhaften Ausblick auf die Bucht von Monaco. • Dans les couloirs des fenêtres en forme de hublot se découpent dans les murs épais. Ils offrent une vue imprenable sur la baie de Monaco.

P. 419 A round table that carries the distinctive signature of the interior designer nestles into the curve at the base of a painted concrete winding stair- case. • Am Fuße der Wendeltreppe aus blau gestrichenem Beton steht ein run- der Tisch, dessen Entwurf von der Desi- gnerin stammt. • Une table ronde qui porte la signature distinctive de la déco-

ratrice se love dans le creux d'un esca- lier à colimaçon en béton peint.

↑ In this room Mahdavi put her signa- ture on most of the furniture. Next to the window we recognise her "Cap Martin" rattan armchair, designed in 2009. • Die meisten Möbelstücke in diesem Zimmer wurden von Mahdavi selbst

entworfen. Vor dem Fenster erkent man ihren Rattan-Sessel „Cap Martin" aus dem Jahr 2009. • Dans cette chambre Mahdavi a apposé sa signature sur la plus grande partie des meubles. Près de la fenêtre, on reconnaît son fauteuil en rotin « Cap Martin » crée en 2009.

P. 421 A table on two levels from the India Mahdavi collection marries perfectly with the curvy form of the sofa. • Der Tisch mit zwei Ebenen aus der Kollektion India Mahdavi passt perfekt zur elegant geschwungenen Form des Sofas. • Une table à deux plateaux de la collection India Mahdavi épouse parfaitement la forme curviligne de la banquette.

↑ The graphic lines of a wall decoration by Aurore de la Morinerie combine harmoniously with the refined shapes of a seat and a table lamp. • Aurore de la Morinerie hat diese grafische Wanddekoration entworfen, die sich harmonisch mit den raffinierten Formen von Sessel und Leuchte verbindet. • Les lignes graphiques d'une décoration murale signée Aurore de la Morinerie se marie à la perfection avec la forme épurée d'un siège et d'une lampe de table.

→ This is an ideal place for a bouquet of white peonies. • Auf dem Tisch hat sich der ideale Ort für ein Bouquet weißer Pfingstrosen gefunden. • Un bouquet de pivoines blanches a trouvé sa place idéale sur une table.

PP. 424–425 In this spacious suite you feel like you are on board a luxurious yacht. Long horizontal bands of colour painted on the walls accentuate the generous dimensions of the room. • Hier fühlt man sich wie an Bord einer Luxus-Yacht! Die großzügigen Dimensionen der Suite werden von langen Farbstreifen entlang der Wände akzentuiert. • Dans cette suite spacieuse, on a l'impression de se trouver à bord d'un yacht luxueux. De longues bandes horizontales peintes sur les murs accentuent les dimensions généreuses de la chambre.

← In a bathroom, the inner porthole above the bath adjoins the lounge. • In einem der Badezimmer gewährt ein Bullauge über der Wanne Einblick ins Wohnzimmer – und umgekehrt. • Dans une salle de bains, le hublot au-dessus de la baignoire est mitoyen avec le séjour.

↑ Vivid yellow triangular tiles cover the walls of the shower room. • Die Wände der Dusche sind mit einem Rautenmuster aus leuchtend gelben Fliesen bedeckt. • Un carrelage jaune vif avec un profil à losanges habille les parois de la douche.

LE CABANON

LE CABANON
CÔTE D'AZUR

The owner of the house must have eyes like a hawk, for he has succeeded in discovering some of the most charming hidden corners of the Côte d'Azur. Even now, he can still remember, down to the last detail, his first encounter with Le Cabanon, an artist's hideaway dating from the end of the 19th century, perched high on a hill with a glorious view of the sea and a distant island. Once he had bought his "lucky find", he was faced with the daunting prospect of adapting the little house to his needs. The burning question was what to do with this tiny single-storey building. Or was it best to go for simplicity and strive to preserve all the authentic detail? When work was completed, he congratulated himself on having made the right choice in treating Le Cabanon as a rather primitive country retreat. It is indeed primitive, but in a positive sense, with chairs radiating old-fashioned charm, a multitude of old lanterns, an ancient garden seat and a rustic Provençal table. The whole arrangement reflects the honest simplicity of a real country cottage, where unpretentious details, such as the blue window frames and shutters, are worth more than all the luxury in the world.

Der Besitzer des Hauses scheint über einen guten Spürsinn zu verfügen, und er hat ein Faible für die schönsten abseits gelegenen Ecken der Côte d'Azur. Noch immer kann er sich an jedes Detail seines ersten Besuchs erinnern. Die ehemalige Künstlerherberge, Ende des 19. Jahrhunderts erbaut, befindet sich auf einem Hügel, der eine wunderbare Aussicht aufs Meer und eine entfernte Insel eröffnet. Als er das Schmuckstück schließlich sein Eigen nennen konnte, begann für ihn eine wahre Sisyphusarbeit, und es stellte sich die Frage, wie das baufällige, einstöckige Haus einzurichten sei. Als die Renovierungsarbeiten endlich abgeschlossen waren, konnte er erleichtert feststellen, dass er gut daran getan hatte, Le Cabanon wie ein einfaches Landhaus einzurichten: ein Sessel von leicht verblichenem Charme, viele alte Laternen, eine schlichte Gartenbank und ein rustikaler, provenzalischer Tisch. Das Ambiente besitzt ländliches Flair, und manche Details, wie der Strauß Geranien in einer Karaffe, die blauen Fensterrahmen und -läden, strahlen – ohne aufgesetzt zu wirken – mehr aus als alle Reichtümer dieser Welt.

Le propriétaire de la maison doit avoir un sixième sens, car il possède un don exceptionnel pour découvrir les plus beaux coins cachés de la Côte d'Azur. Il se souvient encore dans le moindre détail de sa première rencontre avec Le Cabanon, un ancien gîte d'artiste datant de la fin du 19e siècle, perché sur les hauteurs d'une colline et qui offre une vue magnifique sur la mer et sur une île lointaine. Sa trouvaille une fois acquise, il fut confronté à un véritable travail de Sisyphe et à la question brûlante : comment aménager une maisonnette vétuste ? Les travaux terminés, il se félicite d'avoir vu juste et traité Le Cabanon comme une retraite campagnarde un peu primitive. Primitive dans le sens positif du mot, bien sûr, avec des sièges au charme suranné, une multitude de vieilles lanternes, un vieux banc de jardin et une table provençale rustique. L'ensemble émanant l'honnêteté des vraies maisons de campagne et dont certains détails sans prétention – une branche de géranium dans une carafe, des châssis de fenêtre et des volet bleus – valent plus que toutes les richesses du monde.

PP. 428–429 In front of the house, the owner has arranged a fin-de-siècle chaise-longue and a 19th-century concrete garden seat, evoking the sinuous lines of tree trunks and branches. • Vor dem Haus hat der Besitzer eine Liege aus der Zeit des Fin de Siècle und eine Zementbank mit astförmig geschwungenen Streben aus dem 19. Jahrhundert aufgestellt. • Devant le Cabanon le maître de maison a posé une chaise longue fin de siècle et un banc 19ᵉ en ciment qui évoque les formes sinueuses des branches et des troncs d'arbres.

P. 431 Wild vegetation separates the eagle's nest Cabanon from the rocks and the sea. Who would go and search for

a house in this well-hidden place?. • Wie ein Adlernest klebt Le Cabanon am Hang, von Fels und Meer durch wilden Pflanzenwuchs getrennt. Wer würde hier ein Haus suchen wollen?. • Une végétation sauvage sépare le nid d'aigle du Cabanon des rochers et de la mer. Qui irait chercher la présence d'une maison dans ce lieu si bien caché ?

← We always think of the novels of Colette in this landscape; on the terrace you'll discover a wooden trellis that is slowly being overrun by a vine. The real "Muscat grape trellis" of the famous writer is very near … • In dieser Landschaft erinnert man sich oft an die Romane von Colette, und auf der Terrasse findet man

dann eine hölzerne Pergola, von einer Weinrebe umrankt. Die echte „Muskatlaube" der berühmten Schriftstellerin ist nicht weit … • On se souvient toujours des romans de Colette dans ce pays et sur la terrasse on découvre une pergola en bois envahie par la treille d'une vigne. La vraie « Treille Muscate » du célèbre écrivain est très proche.

↑ A potted geranium on a classic ceramic pedestal. • Ein klassizistischer Fayencesockel mit einem Topf Geranien. • Sur un socle en faïence néoclassique un géranium en pot.

PP. 434–435 In the drawing room the rattan armchair and the rustic wooden tables contrast pleasingly with the bright blue-painted Provençal bench and chairs. · Hier bilden ein Korbsessel und schlichte Holzmöbel einen schönen Kontrast zur blauen Bank und den provenzalischen Stühlen. · Dans le salon, le fauteuil en rotin et le mobilier en bois rustique contrastent agréablement avec le banc et les chaises provençales, peintes en bleu vif.

↑ The whitewashed walls and the red-tiled terracotta floor are the perfect setting for robust rustic furniture, a very fine Provençal chair and an amusing

"chinoiserie" lantern. · Weiß gekalkte Wände und Terrakottafliesen harmonieren mit robusten ländlichen Möbeln wie dem sehr schönen provenzalischen Stuhl und der originellen Laterne im China-Stil. · Les murs blanchis à la chaux et le sol garni de tomettes accueillent de robustes meubles campagnards, une très belle chaise provençale et une lanterne frivole, dans le style « chinoiserie ».

→ The same room from a different angle. Here, the owner has arranged a cane table with a wooden top and some unusual metal lanterns. In summer, the straw matting is rolled down over the

door and windows. · Eine weitere Ansicht desselben Raums. Hier hat der Eigentümer einen Korbtisch mit Holzplatte und ungewöhnliche Metalllaternen versammelt. Im Sommer werden die aufgerollten Strohmatten über Tür und Fenster herabgelassen. · La même pièce sous un autre angle. Ici le maître de maison a rassemblé une table en rotin dotée d'un plateau en bois et d'insolites lanternes en métal. En été, les nattes de paille sont déroulées au-dessus de la porte et des fenêtres.

PP. 438–439 A motley group of furniture, consisting of a garden bench, a chair and an armchair, are gathered around the fireplace in the little winter drawing room. It's nice to warm up next to a fire crackling in the hearth. • Wie zufällig zusammengewürfelt stehen die Möbel im kleinen Winterzimmer im Kreis um den Kamin – eine Gartenbank, ein Stuhl und ein Korbsessel. Es ist angenehm, sich vor dem knisternden Feuer aufzuwärmen. • Un mobilier hétéroclite composé d'un banc de jardin, d'une chaise et d'un fauteuil entoure la cheminée dans le petit salon d'hiver. Il est agréable de s'y réchauffer prés du feu qui crépite dans l'âtre.

↑ A few elements are enough to create a pretty still life, and a simple flower in a jug of water is a real pleasure to behold. • Oft genügen wenige Elemente, um ein hübsches Stillleben zu kreieren – eine einzelne Blüte in einem Wasserkrug ist ein Fest für die Augen. • Quelques éléments suffisent pour composer une jolie nature morte et la vue d'une simple fleur dans une carafe à eau est un vrai plaisir pour les yeux.

→ A monastic atmosphere reigns in the bedroom. • Im Schlafzimmer herrscht eine fast klösterliche Atmosphäre. • Dans la chambre à coucher règne une ambiance monacale.

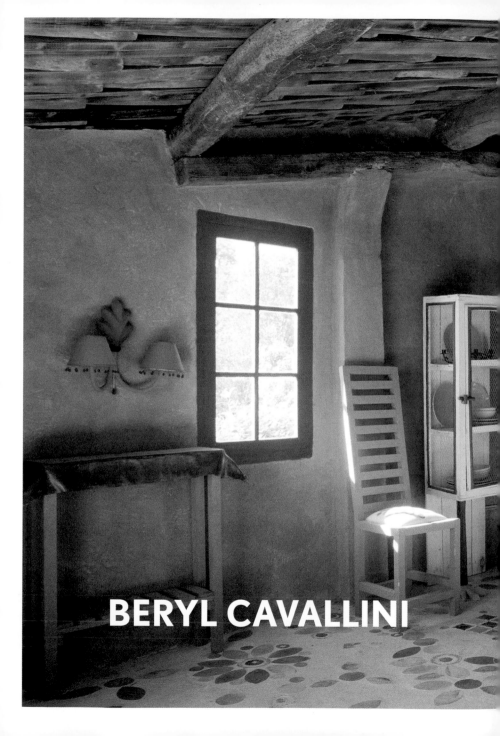
BERYL CAVALLINI

BERYL CAVALLINI
CÔTE D'AZUR

"Indolence" is one of the most beautiful words. In the South of France, it's an art. Deck chairs are arranged beneath the fluttering vines, ready for an icy pastis, a quiet afternoon chat, some murmured observations about the orange tree that will need watering. Bees are buzzing in a tangle of jasmine and the sound is so soothing. The beating of their tiny wings sends eddies of jasmine fragrance into the air, to mingle with the perfumes of orange blossom and rosemary, basil and mint. The bees fly on to fresh fields. Stillness and silence again. It's time for a nap. Sweet summer in the south of France often means a little house affectionately called a "cabanon". And that's what interior designer Beryl Cavallini calls her charming summer retreat. Everything for warm-weather pleasure and fun and comfort is here at hand, from easy chairs, an old tin watering can, sun-ripe oranges, a cool interior to escape to, and a casual bar for convivial gatherings.

„Trägheit" ist ein wunderbares Wort. In Südfrankreich hat man sie zur Kunst erhoben. Liegestühle stehen unter grünen Weinranken bereit für einen eisgekühlten Pastis, eine entspannte Unterhaltung am Nachmittag, ein paar hingemurmelte Bemerkungen über den Orangenbaum, den man mal wieder gießen sollte. Man hört nur das einschläfernde Summen von Bienen, die in den Jasminbüschen umherschwirren. Ihre winzigen Flügel tragen Duftfetzen von Jasmin herüber, die sich mit dem Aroma von Orangenblüten und Rosmarin, Basilikum und Minze vermischen. Dann fliegen die Bienen weiter zu neuen Blüten und es kehrt wieder Stille ein. Zeit für ein Schläfchen. Diese wunderbaren Sommer in Südfrankreich sind oft verbunden mit einem kleinen, liebevoll „cabanon" genannten Landhaus. Und so nennt auch die Interior-Designerin Beryl Cavallini ihr charmantes altes Bauernhaus, wo sie die Sommermonate verbringt. Hier gibt es alles, was man für Sommerspaß, Urlaub und Gemütlichkeit braucht: leichte Gartenstühle, eine alte Zinkgießkanne, sonnengereifte Orangen, kühle Innenräume, die Schutz vor der gleißenden Sonne bieten, und eine Bar für einen entspannten Drink mit Freunden.

« Indolence » est l'un des plus beaux mots du dictionnaire. Dans le Midi de la France, c'est un art. Des transats sont disposés sous une charmille frémissante, prêts pour un pastis glacé, un papotage tranquille d'après-midi, quelques commentaires à mi-voix sur l'oranger qu'il serait peut-être temps d'arroser. On se laisse bercer par un bourdonnement d'abeilles dans un enchevêtrement de jasmin. Les battements de leurs ailes minuscules agitent des effluves fleuries, le jasmin se mêlant au parfum des fleurs d'oranger et du romarin, du basilic et de la menthe. Puis les abeilles partent butiner ailleurs. Le silence et le calme reviennent. C'est l'heure de la sieste. Les doux étés du Midi vont souvent de pair avec ces maisonnettes qu'on appelle affectueusement un « cabanon ». C'est aussi le nom qu'a choisi la décoratrice Beryl Cavallini pour cette vieille bâtisse pleine de charme. Tout ce qu'il faut pour profiter du beau temps, s'amuser et se laisser aller est à portée de main : chaises longues, vieil arrosoir en tôle, oranges gorgées de soleil, intérieurs frais et même un bar improvisé pour recevoir des amis.

PP. 442–443 and 448 Beryl created the coloured patterns in the new concrete floor. They're random, like a dream, and perfect for this dolce far niente cottage. • Beryl gestaltete das Muster auf dem Betonboden selbst. Es besteht aus farbigen Steinen und passt perfekt zum »dolce far niente« von Le Cabanon. • Beryl a créé les motifs de couleur du nouveau sol en ciment. Ils sont aléatoires, comme dans un rêve, et parfaits pour cet antre du dolce far niente.

P. 445 In summer, life revolves around the vine-shaded terrace, the garden, and attending to the trees. Perhaps there are some oranges to pick? • Im Sommer spielt sich das Leben auf der weinumrankten, schattigen Terrasse oder im Garten unter den Bäumen ab. • L'été, la vie évolue autour de la terrasse ombragée, le jardin et les arbres. Peut-être y a-t-il quelques oranges à cueillir?

PP. 446–447 and 449 Hot colours enliven the small kitchen and bar, where rose-coloured walls and a yellow ceiling frame a painting by Walasse Ting. • Kräftige Farben beleben die kleine Küche und die Bar, wo roséfarbene Wände und die gelbe Decke den idealen Rahmen für ein Gemälde von Walasse Ting bilden. • Les couleurs torrides mettent de l'animation dans la petite cuisine-bar, dont les murs roses et le plafond jaune forment un cadre au tableau de Walasse Ting.

AKKO VAN ACKER

AKKO VAN ACKER

CÔTE D'AZUR

It is ages since the famous Dutch antique dealer Akko van Acker began his love affair with the Côte d'Azur. Although he later decided to settle in Paris, he never forgot those wonderful summers and his first shop at Saint-Tropez. Better still, the "Dutch Parisian" soon came across a delightful luxury cottage. There are not too many real "characters" in the world of antiques, but the name of van Acker figures among those famed for their incomparable taste. His style is characterised by a penchant for the "grandiose" and for furniture and objects of generous proportions. Akko loathes anything twee and pretty-pretty and one suspects that the elegant Dutchman's preferences are influenced by the fact that he himself is on the tall side. As you approach the garden, you are met with large statues and architectural fragments. However, the strongest appeal of the garden is its wild, untamed feel. Inside the house, Akko has succeeded in creating the same natural, relaxed atmosphere and there is nothing "recherché" about the decor.

Vor einer halben Ewigkeit verliebte sich der bekannte holländische Kunsthändler Akko van Acker in die Côte d'Azur. Auch als er später in Paris lebte, vergaß er doch nie sein erstes Geschäft und die schönen Sommer in Saint-Tropez. Dort entdeckte der „holländische Pariser" oder „Pariser Holländer" bald ein herrliches Ferienhäuschen. Nur wenige Kunsthändler verfügen über einen ausgeprägten individuellen Stil und exzellenten Geschmack. Zu ihnen zählt mit Sicherheit auch van Acker. Er hat einen Hang zum „Grandiosen" und bevorzugt Möbel mit großzügigen Proportionen. Mittelmäßiges indes ist dem eleganten Holländer ein Greuel, und alles um ihn herum muss seinem Format entsprechen. Überall in seinem Haus im „Midi" begegnet man üppigen Formen, und schon auf dem Weg durch den ungezähmten und verwilderten Garten stößt man auf Statuen und imposante antike Architekturfragmente. Ohne dass es inszeniert wirkt, ist es Akko gelungen, eine ebenso natürliche wie nonchalante Atmosphäre in seinem Haus zu schaffen.

Il y a une éternité, le célèbre antiquaire néerlandais Akko van Acker tomba amoureux de la Côte d'Azur, et même si Akko choisit plus tard de s'établir à Paris, il n'oublia jamais son premier magasin à Saint-Tropez et les beaux étés inondés de soleil. Plus fort encore, le « Hollandais parisien » – ou le « Parisien hollandais » – y dénicha très tôt un beau cabanon de luxe. Les vraies personnalités sont plutôt rares dans le métier d'antiquaire, et parmi ceux qui se sont distingués par leur goût incomparable figure le nom de van Acker. Précisons que son style est caractérisé par un penchant pour le « grandiose » et pour les meubles et les objets aux proportions généreuses. Akko déteste la mièvrerie et on soupçonne que chez ce Hollandais élégant tout doit être à sa taille. Dans sa maison du Midi, les formes généreuses sont omniprésentes ; dès que l'on s'approche du jardin, on est confronté avec des statues et de puissants fragments architecturaux. Pourtant, ce qui séduit le plus dans ce jardin, c'est son côté sauvage et son petit air désinvolte. À l'intérieur, Akko a su évoquer le même naturel et la même nonchalance, et le décor n'a rien de recherché.

PP. 450–451 At Akko van Acker's property, the pool is surrounded by luxuriant vegetation so thick that the whole resembles a virgin Amazonian forest. • Am Anwesen von Akko van Acker ist das Schwimmbecken von blühender Vegetation umgeben – so üppig, dass sie dem Urwald in Amazonien ähnelt. • Dans la propriété d'Akko van Acker, la piscine s'entoure d'une végétation luxuriante et tellement dense que le tout ressemble à une forêt vierge en Amazonie.

P. 453 On the terrace in front of his house, the antiquarian has created a

space destined for relaxation. Surrounded by a jasmine curtain, it has been furnished with old garden benches and a spartan lantern in plaster inspired by Alberto Giacometti. • Die Terrasse vor dem Haus hat der Antiquitätenhändler als einen Ort der Entspannung entworfen. Umgeben von Jasmin, ist sie mit alten Gartenbänken ausgestattet und einem dürren, von Alberto Giacometti inspirierten Lüster – aus Gips. • Sur la terrasse, devant sa maison, l'antiquaire a créé un espace destiné à la détente. Entouré d'un rideau de jasmin, il a été meublé avec des vieux bancs de jardin

et un lustre squelette en plâtre inspiré par Alberto Giacometti.

← Akko has decorated his garden with numerous finds. The Roman throne and a large obelisk betray his taste for everything that concerns antiquity. • Seinen Garten dekoriert Akko mit seinen Funden, der römische Thron und ein hoher Obelisk geben Einblick in seine Vorliebe für die Antike. • Akko a décoré son jardin avec ses nombreuses trouvailles. Le « trône » romain et la grande obélisque trahissent son goût pour tout ce qui touche à l'Antiquité.

P. 455 On the terrace a wrought iron table and enamelled Anduze vases have managed to settle in among the abundant vegetation. • Auf der Terrasse finden der schmiedeeiserne Tisch und die glasierten Anduze-Vasen ihren Platz inmitten der Vegetation. • Sur la terrasse, une table en fer forgé et des vases d'Anduze émaillés ont réussi à trouver une place parmi la végétation abondante.

↑ A stone elephant adds an exotic note in the "wild" part of the garden. • Ein steinerner Elefant gibt dem „wilden" Teil des Gartens eine exotische Note. • Un éléphant en pierre ajoute une note exotique dans la partie « sauvage » du jardin.

→ The painted terracotta cherub emerging from a flowering bush has seen better days... • Dieses bemalte Engelein aus Terrakotta, das aus einem Strauch hervorlugt, ist wahrscheinlich nicht mehr ganz jung ... • Le chérubin en terre cuite peinte qui émerge d'un buisson fleuri a vu de meilleurs jours...

↑ In the untamed garden, a pergola almost disappears beneath the weight of overgrown foliage. • Im Garten befindet sich eine Laube, die dem Blattdickicht kaum gewachsen ist. • Le jardin sauvage est doté d'une pergola qui s'effondre sous le poids du feuillage envahissant.

→ An old studded door gives access to the garden and bars the way to the curious. • Eine alte, mit Eisennägeln bewehrte Tür öffnet sich zum Garten – wenn sie will. • Une très ancienne porte cloutée donne accès au jardin et barre le chemin aux curieux.

→ A superb Regency mirror hangs above the drawing room's Louis XV fireplace. • Im großen Salon hat der Kunsthändler über dem Louis-XV-Kamin einen wunderbaren Régence-Spiegel angebracht. • Dans le grand salon, l'antiquaire a accroché un superbe miroir Régence au-dessus de la cheminée Louis XV.

← The magnificent Baroque furniture at the back of the drawing room comes from an old Italian pharmacy and dates from the early 18th century. • Das herrliche barocke Möbel im Salon stammt aus einer italienischen Apotheke und ist Anfang des 18. Jahrhunderts entstanden. • Le magnifique meuble baroque dans le fond du salon provient d'une ancienne pharmacie en Italie. Il date du début du 18e siècle.

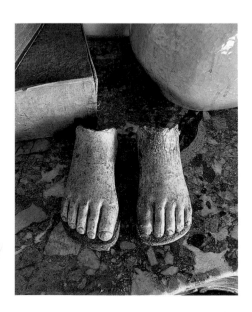

↑ On the books, Akko has placed a dried rose, a gift from a late friend. • Auf den Büchern liegt eine getrocknete Rose, das Geschenk einer verstorbenen Freundin. • Sur les livres, Akko a posé une rose séchée, cadeau d'une amie regrettée.

← Two little terracotta feet from the Roman era have finally come to rest on a console. • Auf einer Konsole haben zwei kleine tönerne Füße aus römischer Zeit ihren Platz gefunden. • Sur une console, deux petits pieds en terre cuite d'époque romaine ont enfin trouvé le repos.

LA BUISSAIE

LA BUISSAIE
CÔTE D'AZUR

As you pass alongside La Buissaie, you see a rough stone wall covered with ivy and, beyond it, you catch no more than a glimpse of a few windows with blue shutters. Just what you expect when you conjure up the idea of a romantic house set in a mature garden. La Buissaie fits the image to perfection. This modest, early 19th-century house, in its enchanting garden, is the stuff of nostalgic dreams. Look at the hallway with its yellow ochre walls and its spiral staircase. Walk into the kitchen with its blue-and-white tiles, blue shutters and round table with its chequered cloth. The theatre director and set designer who bought the property were both captivated by the blue shutters and stone fireplaces, the red-tiled floors and the old fountain. For the new owners of La Buissaie, it was an opportunity to practise their craft and create a home to live in. As they like to keep things simple, they only added a few old pieces of furniture and unpretentious bits and pieces picked up in secondhand shops. The result is a house full of colour and fragrant smells, where blue and ochre, green and white intermingle with the scent of thyme, savory, lavender and rosemary.

Steht man vor La Buissaie, so fallen zunächst die efeubewachsenen Mauern auf, und jenseits davon lassen sich einige Fenster mit blauen Läden ausmachen. Dieses schlichte Landhaus aus dem frühen 19. Jahrhundert entspricht mit seinem herrlichen Garten genau der Vorstellung, die man sich gemeinhin von einem romantischen Haus macht. Man betrachte nur den ockergelben Hausflur mit der Wendeltreppe oder die blau-weiß-gekachelte Küche mit den blauen Fenster-läden, der karierten Tischdecke … Die Besitzer dieses Anwesens, ein Regisseur und ein Bühnenbildner, waren beson-ders von den blauen Fensterläden, den Kaminen, den Terrakottafliesen und dem alten Brunnen angetan. In gewisser Weise kommt den neuen Eigentümern von La Buissaie ihr Beruf entgegen, können sie hier ein Haus doch geradezu inszenieren. Da beide das Einfache lieben, richteten sie ihr Haus mit einigen alten Möbeln und Fundstücken vom Flohmarkt ein. Sie schufen ein Ambiente voller Farben und Düfte, in dem Blau und Ocker, Grün und Weiß mit den wür-zigen Gerüchen von Thymian, Bohnenkraut, Lavendel und Rosmarin harmonieren.

En passant devant La Buissaie, on voit un mur en grosses pierres couvert de lierre, et au-delà de ce mur on distingue à peine quelques fenêtres aux volets bleus. Tout juste ce qu'il faut pour faire naître l'image d'une maison romantique et de son vieux jardin. La Buissaie répond parfaitement à cette image. Entourée d'un ravissant jardin, cette modeste maison de campagne datant du début du 19ᵉ siècle a tout pour plaire aux âmes nostalgiques. Regardez l'entrée avec ses murs ocre jaune et son escalier en colimaçon et entrez dans la cuisine avec ses murs carrelés bleu et blanc, ses volets assortis et sa table ronde revêtue d'une nappe à carreaux … Le metteur en scène et le décorateur de théâtre qui ont acheté la propriété ont été charmés par les volets, les cheminées en pierre, les sols en tomettes et la vieille fontaine. En quelque sorte, les nouveaux maîtres de La Buissaie allaient pouvoir exercer leur métier et mettre en scène une vraie maison. Comme ils aiment la simplicité, ils ont garni la maison de quelques vieux meubles et de trouvailles sans prétention déni-chées chez les brocanteurs. Et voilà une maison composée de couleurs et de parfums, où le bleu et l'ocre, le vert et le blanc se marient à l'arôme du thym, de la sarriette, de la lavande et du romarin.

PP. 464–465 La Buissaie is hidden behind a stone wall covered with ivy and oleander. • La Buissaie verbirgt sich hinter einer Steinmauer, die dicht mit Efeu und Oleander bewachsen ist. • La Buissaie se cache derrière un mur en pierre couvert de lierre et de laurier-rose.

P. 467 One of the masters of the house enjoys a well-deserved moment of relaxation. • Einer der beiden Haus-

herren bei einer wohlverdienten Ruhe-pause. • Un des maîtres de maison, savourant un repos bien mérité.

← A very old covered terrace provides protection for firewood as well as a dining area. • Die Überdachung der alten Terrasse schützt das Kaminholz und die Essecke. • Une très ancienne terrasse couverte abrite le bois de chauffage et un coin-repas.

↑ Tall, clipped hedges, avalanches of ivy and masses of oleander transform the garden into a veritable jungle. • Hohe Buchsbaumhecken und eine Fülle von Efeu und Oleander verwandeln den Garten in einen wahren Dschungel. • De hautes haies en buis taillé, des avalanches de lierre et des massifs de laurier-rose transforment le jardin en une véritable jungle.

← Blue and white are the predominant colours in the kitchen. The walls are tiled and a "banquette" has been built into the alcove. • In der Küche dominieren Blau und Weiß. Die Wände sind gekachelt, im Alkoven wurde eine Sitzbank eingerichtet. • Dans la cuisine, le bleu et le blanc dominent. Les murs sont carrelés, et l'alcôve abrite une banquette encastrée.

↑ The hall and stairwell have been colour-washed in yellow ochre. The console is an "artistic" composition by the two owners, while the metal wall lamps and the mirror were unearthed in secondhand shops. • Flur und Treppenhaus wurden ockergelb gestrichen. Eine „Schöpfung" der Hausbesitzer ist die Konsole, während die

Metalllampen und der Spiegel Fundstücke vom Flohmarkt sind. • L'entrée et la cage d'escalier ont été badigeonnées d'ocre jaune. La console est une création « artistique » des habitants, les appliques en tôle et le miroir ont été trouvés chez les brocanteurs.

← The spiral staircase leads to the first floor and attic. • Die Wendeltreppe führt zum ersten Stock und auf den Speicher. • L'escalier en colimaçon dessert l'étage et le grenier.

↑ From the first-floor landing, a blue door opens into the bedroom with its red terracotta floor tiles. • Vom Treppenabsatz im ersten Stock aus fällt der Blick auf die blaue Tür, die in das mit Terrakottaplatten geflieste Schlafzimmer führt. • Sur le palier du premier étage, on aperçoit la porte bleue qui s'ouvre sur la chambre à coucher et le sol couvert de tomettes.

JEAN-PAUL THOMAS

JEAN-PAUL THOMAS
CÔTE D'AZUR

It began as a modest cottage with just one room, surrounded by a small plot of land. But what attracted make-up artist Jean-Paul Thomas to the little house was its location, perched like an eagle's nest on a rocky promontory, with a view of the sea and one of the Côte d'Azur's most picturesque bays. Thomas is a straightforward kind of chap, and while, professionally, he moves in the world of fashion and theatre, all he really wants is a quiet life. In Paris, he has to decide what colour cosmetics women will wear, but here on the coast he prefers to spend time transforming his "little hut". With the help of his friend Frédéric Méchiche, the famous interior designer, he has transformed the tiny square building into a house with pure, classic lines, but even if the accent is on simplicity and austerity, the place has lost none of its welcoming atmosphere. Of course, along with the owner's favourite objects, like photos, watercolours and still lifes made from shells, there are plenty of typical Méchiche touches. A whole series of aesthetically pleasing and well-chosen bits and pieces have turned this simple little house into an enviable place to live.

Ursprünglich gab es auf dem knapp bemessenen Grundstück nur ein kleines Haus mit einem einzigen Zimmer, doch der Visagist Jean-Paul Thomas war von der Lage begeistert: dem Blick aus einem Adlerhorst vergleichbar eröffnet sich hier freie Sicht auf das Meer und eine der schönsten Buchten der Côte d'Azur. Thomas ist ein gradliniger Mensch, und obwohl ihn sein Beruf ständig in die turbulente Welt der Mode und des Theaters führt, träumt er eigentlich von einem ruhigen Leben. In Paris entscheidet er mit, welches Make-up die Frauenwelt demnächst trägt, an der Côte d'Azur kümmert er sich lieber um die Verschönerung seiner „Hütte". Dabei kommt ihm seine enge Freundschaft mit dem berühmten Innenarchitekten Frédéric Méchiche sehr zugute. Ohne dessen Talent hätte die Vergrößerung des Häuschens ein Fehlschlag werden können, und das niedliche quadratische Gebäude wäre vielleicht völlig verbaut worden. Mittlerweile wurde es in ein Haus mit klaren klassischen Linien verwandelt. Natürlich finden sich hier viele Einflüsse von Méchiche, aber die Lieblingsobjekte des Hausherrn, wie Fotos, Aquarelle oder Stillleben aus Muscheln, sind nicht zu übersehen. Viele geschmackvolle Fundstücke tragen mit dazu bei, aus einer Hütte ein bewundernswertes Zuhause zu machen.

Au début ce n'était qu'une modeste maison d'une seule pièce entouré d'un bout de terrain aux dimensions réduites, mais ce qui séduisait le visagiste Jean-Paul Thomas, c'était sa position en « nid d'aigle » perché sur un promontoire rocheux et la vue qu'il offrait sur la mer et sur une des baies les plus pittoresques de la Côte d'Azur. Thomas est un homme sans détours, et si de par son métier il fréquente le monde de la mode et du théâtre, il ne rêve en réalité que d'une vie calme. À Paris, c'est lui qui décide de la gamme de couleurs qui embellira les « stars », mais sur la Côte il préfère s'occuper des transformations de son « cagibi ». Jean-Paul a un grand avantage : il est très ami avec Frédéric Méchiche, le célèbre architecte d'intérieur ; il est d'ailleurs prêt à avouer que sans le talent de Méchiche, l'agrandissement de son cabanon aurait pu tourner au désastre, que la minuscule bâtisse carrée aurait pu se transformer en un hybride bizarre. Aujourd'hui elle s'est métamorphosée en une maison aux lignes pures et classiques. Bien sûr, nous y trouvons plein d'accents typiquement Méchiche, mais aussi les objets préférés du maître de maison, tels que des photos, des aquarelles et des natures mortes en coquillages, qui ont transformé ce cabanon en une demeure enviable.

PP. 474–475 In the much-extended living room, Frédéric Méchiche has been able to exploit the delicate design of antique garden furniture and some 19th-century chairs. He also designed the rounded windows. • Den beträchtlich erweiterten Wohnraum möblierte Méchiche mit einer wunderbaren Auswahl alter Gartenmöbel und Sessel aus dem 19. Jahrhundert. Die Rundbogenfenster hat er selbst entworfen. • Dans le séjour considérablement agrandi, Frédéric Méchiche a pu tirer le meilleur parti du dessin délicat des anciens meubles de jardin et de quelques sièges 19ᵉ. Les fenêtres arrondies portent également sa signature.

P. 477 A plateau close to the house provides a panoramic viewpoint. • Ein Plateau in der Nähe des Hauses dient als Aussichtspunkt. • Près de la propriété, un plateau sert de belvédère.

→ In the drawing room, a sofa bed is covered with unbleached linen. The little octagonal tea table is from Morocco. • Ein Schlafsofa im Wohnzimmer ist mit rohem Leinen bezogen. Der kleine, achteckige Teetisch stammt aus Marokko. • Dans le séjour un canapé-lit a été recouvert avec une housse en coton écru. La petite table à thé octogonale est d'origine Marocaine.

↑ On the mantlepiece Jean-Paul has assembled a charming still life around a very fine portrait of the late Danielle Darrieux by Raymond Voinquel. • Auf dem Kaminsims hat Jean-Paul ein apartes Stilleben arrangiert, im Vordergrund ein Porträt der kürzlich verstorbenen Danielle Darrieux des Fotografen Raymond Voinquel. • Sur la tablette de la cheminée, Jean-Paul a composé une charmante nature morte dominée par un très beau portrait de feu Danielle Darrieux par Raymond Voinquel.

→ The presence of an old print and a neoclassical bronze candlestick converted into a table lamp are signs of the influence of Frédéric Méchiche. • Ein alter Stich und ein neo-klassizistischer Leuchter aus Bronze, nun eine Tischlampe, verraten den Einfluss von Frédéric Méchiche. • La présence d'une gravure ancienne et d'un candélabre en bronze néo-classique transformé en lampe de table trahit l'influence de Frédéric Méchiche.

← Jean-Paul Thomas creates colour ranges for the cosmetics industry, but in his bathroom he has restricted himself to grey-blue and... black and white. • Jean-Paul entwirft Farbpaletten für die Kosmetik, aber im Bad dominieren Grau und Blau und ... Schwarz-Weiß. • Jean-Paul Thomas crée des gammes de couleurs pour l'industrie cosmétique mais dans sa salle de bains il s'est limité en choisissant du gris-bleu et...du noir et blanc.

↑ In his bedroom, Jean-Paul has installed a little office corner in case inspiration comes to him in the middle of the night. • Im Schlafzimmer hat Jean-Paul einen kleinen Arbeitstisch aufgestellt, falls die Inspiration ihn mitten in der Nacht überkommt. • Dans sa chambre, Jean-Paul a installé un petit coin bureau au cas où l'inspiration lui viendrait au beau milieu de la nuit.

JEANNE &
JEAN-MARIE
MARÉCHAL

JEANNE &
JEAN-MARIE MARÉCHAL
PROVENCE, ON THE ROAD

Every young child entertains the eternal and romantic dream of running away with the gypsies. It's a mythological flight from convention and restrictions, to a fantasy of life-without-care on the open road. Gypsies (Roma), originally from northwest India and itinerant by choice, have roamed Europe, England and Ireland since the 11th century. In the early 19th century, they began to travel from town to town in painted wagons. Few of these ornate wagons are still in existence today, superseded by modern vehicles. In Provence, Jeanne and Jean-Marie Maréchal fell in love with traditional folkloric gypsy wagons ("les roulottes" in French) and have made rescuing and restoring these cultural relics a mission and their life's work. Jeanne noted that many caravans have simply been destroyed over time, while others were ritually burned upon the death of a Roma patriarch. The Maréchals repaint the old wagons with vivid colours and allegorical imagery.

Träumt nicht jedes Kind einmal davon, auf große Fahrt zu gehen, mit einem Zigeunerwagen auf und davon? Es ist eine Art mythologischer Flucht vor den Konventionen und Grenzen des Alltags, hin zu einem Leben auf der Straße, ohne Sorgen und Zwänge. Die Roma stammen ursprünglich aus Nordwestindien, bereits im 11. Jahrhundert wanderten sie durch Europa. Im frühen 19. Jahrhundert begannen sie, in bunt bemalten Wagen von Stadt zu Stadt zu ziehen. Heute gibt es nur noch wenige dieser reich verzierten Wagen, die meisten wurden von modernen Fahrzeugen abgelöst. Jeanne und Jean-Marie Maréchal verliebten sich in die traditionellen Zigeunerwagen der Provence, die „roulottes" genannt werden, und machten es zu ihrer Lebensaufgabe, diese kulturellen Schätze zu retten und zu restaurieren. Viele Wohnwagen sind einfach mit der Zeit kaputtgegangen, oder, so erzählt Jeanne, wurden nach dem Tod eines Roma-Patriarchen verbrannt. Die Maréchals bemalen die alten Wohnwagen wieder mit den traditionellen allegorischen Bildern in kräftigen Farben.

Tous les jeunes enfants nourrissent le rêve éternel et romantique de s'enfuir avec les romanichels. C'est une fuite mythologique loin des conventions et des restrictions, vers une vie imaginaire de vagabondage sans soucis. Les Tziganes, venus à l'origine du nord de l'Inde et nomades par choix, sillonnent l'Europe, l'Angleterre et l'Irlande depuis le 11ᵉ siècle. Au début du 19ᵉ siècle, ils se mirent à voyager de ville en ville dans des carrioles peintes et ouvragées. Aujourd'hui, ces dernières ont été supplantées par les véhicules modernes mais il en subsiste encore quelques-unes. En Provence, Jeanne et Jean-Marie Maréchal sont tombés sous le charme de ces roulottes traditionnelles et ont fait de la sauvegarde et de la restauration de ces reliques culturelles leur mission. De nombreuses caravanes sont tombées en poussière avec le temps, alors que d'autres ont été rituellement brûlées à la mort d'un patriarche. Les Maréchal ont repeint les vieilles roulottes avec leurs couleurs vives et leur iconographie allégorique traditionnelles.

PP. 484–485 The inside of the caravan features two dressers for storage,
a raised bed and a small wood-burning
stove. The lace curtains at the windows
are typical of gypsy interiors. • Im In-
nern des Wohnwagens befinden sich
zwei Schränke, ein erhöhtes Bett und ein
kleiner Holzofen. Die Spitzenvorhänge
vor den Fenstern sind typisch für Zigeunerwagen. • L'intérieur de la roulotte
comporte deux commodes pour le ran-
gement, un lit surélevé et un petit poêle
à charbon. Les rideaux en dentelle sont
typiques des intérieurs gitans.

PP. 487 and 488 Jeanne and Jean-
Marie Maréchal redecorated their small

green gypsy wagon in the spirit of southern France to depict a life of ease and
gaiety. Using vibrant colours like red,
blue and green and vintage flowered
fabrics, they restored the wagon to its
original splendour. • Leicht und heiter:
Jeanne und Jean-Marie Maréchal richteten ihren kleinen grünen Zigeunerwagen im südfranzösischen Stil ein. Sie
verwendeten kräftige Farben wie Rot,
Blau und Grün und gaben mit alten ge-
blümten Stoffen dem Wagen seinen ursprünglichen Glanz zurück. • Jeanne et
Jean-Marie Maréchal ont redécoré leur
petite roulotte de gitan verte dans l'esprit du Midi de la France, symbole d'une
vie gaie et facile. À l'aide de rouges, de

bleus et de verts énergiques et de tissus
anciens à fleurs, ils lui ont fait retrouver
sa splendeur d'antan.

→ Entirely constructed of wooden
planks and painted entirely in vibrant
colours, gypsy caravans are a treat for
the eye. • Aus Holz gebaut und über
und über in lebendigen Farben bemalt,
sind die alten Zigeunerwagen ein Fest
fürs Auge. • Entièrement construites en
planches de bois et entièrement peintes
dans des couleurs éclatantes, les roulottes des gitans sont un vrai plaisir pour
les yeux.

← The Maréchals also collect old and rare books about their favourite subject: the adventurous lives of gypsies all over the world. • Das Ehepaar sammelt alte und wertvolle Bücher zu seinem Interessensgebiet: das abenteuerliche Leben der Roma überall auf der Welt. • Les Maréchal collectionnent aussi des livres

anciens qui traitent de leur sujet préféré : l'existence aventureuse des gitans du monde entier.

↑ Maybe it's pure coincidence but the bold colours of the caravan walls are also found in the flowery fabric of the skirt stool cover. • Vielleicht ein Zufall. Die

prächtigen Farben der Wände finden sich im Blumenmuster des Stoffes wieder, der den Hocker überzieht . • Il se peut que ce soit une pure coïncidence mais on retrouve les couleurs franches sur les murs de la roulotte dans le tissu à fleurs du tabouret juponné.

← The decoration surrounding the alcove has a spontaneous, instinctive character untrammelled by the dictates of so-called "good taste". • Der Schlafalkoven wurde spontan dekoriert, ganz nach Gefühl und frei von den Überlegungen des sogenannten guten Geschmacks. • L'alcôve dans laquelle on dort s'entoure d'une décoration sponta-

née et instinctive qui n'est pas entravée par la dictature du soi-disant bon goût.

↑ A very handsome old tablecloth covers the little dining table. The venerated image of the Virgin protects caravan residents from the evil eye. • Der Esstisch wird von einer hübschen, altmodischen Decke geschmückt, und ein Bild

der Muttergottes soll die Bewohner des Wohnwagens vor dem „bösen Blick" schützen. • Un très beau tapis de table ancien recouvre la table sur laquelle on prend les repas. L'image pieuse de la Sainte Vierge protège les habitants de la roulotte du mauvais œil.

← Above the sofa bed, a picture of St. Thérèse of Lisieux has a pretty guilt frame. The round cushions are from the 1930s. • Über dem Kanapee ein Bild der Heiligen Therese von Lisieux, in Gold gerahmt. Die runden Kissen stammen noch aus den Dreißigerjahren. • Au-dessus du canapé-lit Sainte-Thérèse de Lisieux s'entoure d'un joli cadre doré. Les coussins ronds datent des années trente.

↑ Gypsies have a strong faith, and in their caravans they would not be able to live without the divine presence of the mother of Jesus. • Die Zigeuner sind sehr gläubig, und in ihren Wohnmobilen könnten sie nicht ohne die Anwesenheit der Mutter Gottes leben. • Les gitans sont très croyants et dans leur roulotte ils ne sauraient se passer de la présence divine de la mère de Jésus.

PP. 496–497 Who wouldn't like to live in a colourful caravan, free of the constraints of modern life and with no care for what others might say about matters of decor? • Wer würde nicht gern in einem bunt bemalten Wagen wohnen wollen, den Sorgen der modernen Welt enthoben und ohne sich um die Geschmacksurteile der anderen kümmern zu müssen? • Qui n'aimerait pas vivre dans une roulotte bariolée, libre des contraintes de la vie moderne et sans se soucier du « qu'en dira-t-on » en matière de décoration ?

Tuscan treasures

Gorgeous homes in the Italian countryside

Cypress-lined avenues, medieval villas, and orange blossoms:
step into some of the most beautiful havens of Tuscany. Grand patrician
homes and rural hermitages alike open their doors to reveal Medici pottery,
sun-kissed drawing rooms, antique frescoes, and colorful tiled floors.
With detailed captions and crisp photography, this portfolio presents each
home and its interior to paint a gorgeous picture of Tuscan living.

"A thoroughly
absorbing piece
of escapism."

— *The Italian Magazine*, London

Living in Tuscany
Angelika Taschen, Barbara & René Stoeltie
472 pages

TRILINGUAL EDITIONS IN:
ENGLISH / DEUTSCH / FRANÇAIS &
ESPAÑOL / ITALIANO / PORTUGUÊS

In a world without walls

Balinese homes in harmony with nature

Carved wood, secluded courtyards, and frangipani blossoms: soak up the Eastern elegance of these heavenly Indonesian interiors. Opening onto gorgeous green landscapes, majestic mountains, or beautiful coastlines, these Balinese homes exude relaxing, contemplative vibes. Unwind and refresh with this compact showcase of rustic paradises, updated with fresh, never-before-seen images.

"A feast of color, exquisite décor and peaceful presence."

— *Style Magazine*, Cape Town

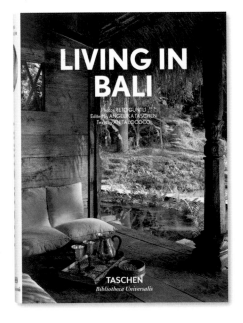

Living in Bali
Reto Guntli, Anita Lococo,
Angelika Taschen
472 pages

TRILINGUAL EDITIONS IN:
ENGLISH / DEUTSCH / FRANÇAIS &
ESPAÑOL / ITALIANO / PORTUGUÊS

YOU CAN FIND TASCHEN STORES IN

Amsterdam
P.C. Hooftstraat 44

Berlin
Schlüterstr. 39

Beverly Hills
354 N. Beverly Drive

Brussels
Rue Lebeaustraat 18

Cologne
Neumarkt 3

Hamburg
Bleichenbrücke 1-7

Hollywood
Farmers Market,
6333 W. 3rd Street, CT-10

Hong Kong
Shop G02, Block 1,
Tai Kwun,
10 Hollywood Road,
Central

London
12 Duke of York Square

London Claridge's
49 Brook Street

Miami
1111 Lincoln Rd.

Milan
Via Meravigli 17

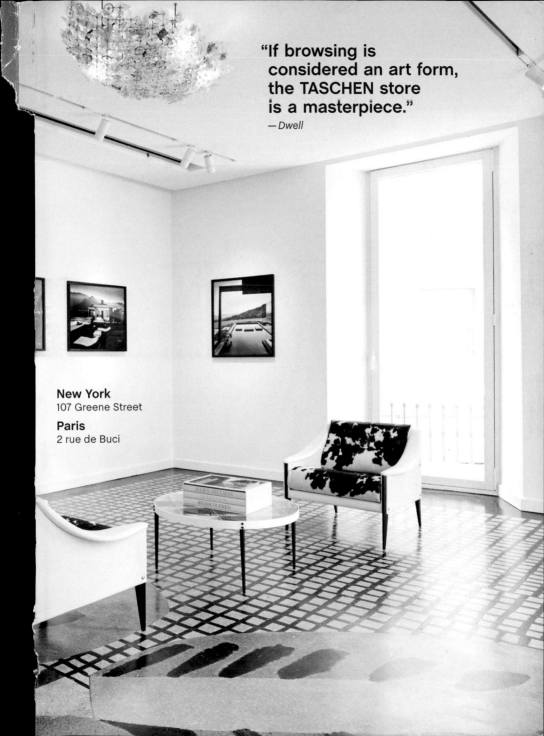

Château de Massillan: pp. 10–19, Barbara and René Stoeltie **Emmanuel de Sauvebœuf**: pp. 20–31, Barbara and René Stoeltie **L'Hôtel Particulier**: pp. 32–41, Barbara and René Stoeltie **Grand Hôtel Nord-Pinus**: pp. 42–51, Barbara and René Stoeltie **Le Cloître**: pp. 52–63, François Halard **La Mirande**: pp. 64–87, Barbara and René Stoeltie (p. 67, 68, 70, 74, 75, 76/77, 78, 79, 83), Guy Hervais (64/65, 69, 71, 72/73, 80, 81, 82, 84, 85, 86, 87) **Laurence Rigaill & Cyril Jean**: pp. 88–99, Marco Tassinari **Michelle & Yves Halard**: pp. 100–119, Barbara and René Stoeltie (103, 104, 105, 107, 109, 112/113), François Halard, Trunk Archive, NY (100/101, 106, 108, 110, 111, 114, 115, 116/117, 118, 119) **House of Frédéric Mistral**: pp. 120–129, Barbara and René Stoeltie **L'Hôtel de Bournissac**: pp. 130–137, Barbara and René Stoeltie **La Maison Domaine de Bournissac**: pp. 138–149, Eric Laignel **Jean Claude Brialy**: pp. 150–157, Barbara and René Stoeltie **Château des Alpilles**: pp. 158–169, all photos supplied by the hotel (Gilles Martin-Raget) **Le Mas d'Esto**: pp. 170–181, Barbara and René Stoeltie **La Bastide**: pp. 182–203, Barbara and René Stoeltie **La Maison Roque**: pp. 204–213, Barbara and René Stoeltie **Jas de L'Ange**: pp. 214–225, Barbara and René Stoeltie **John Burningham & Helen Oxenbury**: pp. 226–233, Barbara and René Stoeltie **La Bastide de Marie**: pp. 234–247, Guy Hervais & Philippe Seuilliet **Une Maison Troglodyte**: pp. 248–257, Barbara and René Stoeltie **La Grande Bégude**: pp. 258–267, Barbara and René Stoeltie **Jean & Dorothée d'Orgeval**: pp. 268–277, Barbara and René Stoeltie **L'Atelier des Lauves**: pp. 278–291, Barbara and René Stoeltie **Château de Cassis**: pp. 292–313, COTE SUD, H. del Olmo **Frédéric Méchiche**: pp. 314–337, Barbara and René Stoeltie **Villa Marie**: pp. 338–347, Villa Marie/L. Di Orio, C. Larit, HKV & DR, Guillaume de Laubier, www.guillaumedelaubier.com (pp. 341, 343) **Villa Bellevue**: pp. 348–357, Barbara and René Stoeltie **Pierre Cardin**: pp. 358–367, Matthew Hranek/gigiamarchiori.com **Pastis Hôtel St Tropez**: pp. 368–375, supplied by the hotel (Oliver Durey p. 375) **Hôtel du Cap-Eden-Roc**: pp. 376–389, Guillaume de Laubier, www.guillaumedelaubier.com, supplied by the hotel (p. 378) **Cap Estel**: pp. 390–407, all photos supplied by the hotel **Monte-Carlo Beach**: pp. 408–427, Daniel Schäfer/TASCHEN GmbH, www.danielschaeferphoto.com **Le Cabanon**: pp. 428–441, Barbara and René Stoeltie **Beryl Cavallini**: pp. 442–449, Giulio Oriani/VEGA MG **Akko van Acker**: pp. 450–463, Barbara and René Stoeltie **La Buissaie**: pp. 464–473, Barbara and René Stoeltie **Jean-Paul Thomas**: pp. 474–483, Barbara and René Stoeltie **Jeanne & Jean-Marie Maréchal**: pp. 484–509, Giulio Oriani/VEGA MG

We have neither the words nor the space to express our deep gratitude to all those who so warmly welcomed us during our trips to Provence. We would, however, like to make special mention of the hospitality offered by France Louis-Dreyfus, Jean-Claude Brialy, Timothy Hennessy, Siki de Somalie, the Stein family, John Burningham and Helen Oxenbury. We would also like to thank Michel Fraisset and the town council of Maillane, who gave us free access to Cézanne's atelier and to the house of Frédéric Mistral. Thanks to them, "Lou souléou me fai canta" (the sun makes me sing).

Uns fehlen die Worte und auch der Platz, um allen zu danken, die uns während unseres Provence-Aufenthalts so herzlich empfangen haben. Dennoch möchten wir die Gastfreundschaft von France Louis-Dreyfus, Jean-Claude Brialy, Timothy Hennessy, Siki de Somalie, der Familie Stein, John Burningham und Helen Oxenbury nicht verschweigen. Dank gebührt auch Michel Fraisset und dem Bürgermeisteramt in Maillane, die uns den Zugang zu Cézannes Atelier und zu dem Haus von Frédéric Mistral ermöglicht haben. Dank ihres Entgegenkommens „Lou souléou me fai canta" (Die Sonne brachte mich zum Singen).

Les mots et l'espace nous font défaut pour exprimer notre gratitude à tous ceux qui nous ont chaleureusement accueillis pendant nos séjours en Provence. Nous ne pouvons toutefois omettre de mentionner l'hospitalité que nous ont offerte France Louis-Dreyfus, Jean-Claude Brialy, Timothy Hennessy, Siki de Somalie, la famille Stein, John Burningham et Helen Oxenbury, et de remercier Michel Fraisset et la Mairie de Maillane qui nous ont donné libre accès à l'atelier de Cézanne et à la maison de Frédéric Mistral. Grâce à eux, « Lou souléou me fai canta ».

Barbara & René Stoeltie

IMPRINT

EACH AND EVERY TASCHEN BOOK PLANTS A SEED!

TASCHEN is a carbon neutral publisher. Each year, we offset our annual carbon emissions with carbon credits at the Instituto Terra, a reforestation program in Minas Gerais, Brazil, founded by Lélia and Sebastião Salgado. To find out more about this ecological partnership, please check: www.taschen.com/zerocarbon
Inspiration: unlimited. Carbon footprint: zero.

To stay informed about TASCHEN and our upcoming titles, please subscribe to our free magazine at www.taschen.com/magazine, follow us on Twitter, Instagram and Facebook, or e-mail your questions to contact@taschen.com.

EDITING
Angelika Taschen, Berlin

PROJECT MANAGEMENT
Stephanie Paas and Daria Razumovych, Cologne

DESIGN
Birgit Eichwede, Cologne

LAYOUT
Tanja da Silva, Cologne

PRODUCTION
Tina Ciborowius, Cologne

TEXTS BY
Barbara and René Stoeltie, Shelley-Maree Cassidy, Ian Phillips, Max Scharnigg, Christiane Reiter, Kristin Rübesamen, Julia Strauß, Diane Dorrans Saeks

ENGLISH TRANSLATION
Julie Street, Iain Reynolds, Anthony Roberts, Isabel Varea, Robert Taylor, Hazel Britton for LocTeam, Barcelona

GERMAN TRANSLATION
Birgit Lamerz-Beckschäfer, Claudia Egdorf, Sabine Gugetzer, Franca Fritz & Heinrich Koop, Stefan Barmann, Marion Valentin, Sybille Schlegel-Bulloch, Ingrid Hacker-Klier, Kornelia Stuckenberger, Sebastian Hau

FRENCH TRANSLATION
Delphine Nègre-Bouvet, Philippe Safavi, Sabine Boccador, Cécile Carrion

PAGE 2 Some sprigs of lavender in an old wicker basket make a charming bouquet.

PAGE 6 It wouldn't be a genuine Provençal garden without the gentle murmuring of water in an old drinking trough.

PAGE 8 An arrangement of shells, coral branches and starfish inspired an old master.

© 2018 for the works of Jean-Charles Blais

© 2018 TASCHEN GmbH
Hohenzollernring 53, D–50672 Köln
www.taschen.com

Original edition: © 2005 TASCHEN GmbH

Printed in Poland
ISBN 978-3-8365-7286-6